Faces and Figures in Embroidery

Faces and Figures in Embroidery

VALERIE HARDING

Charles T. Branford Company Newton Centre, Mass.

Contents

Acknowledgment

I would like to thank Jan Beaney and her City and Guilds class at the Windsor and Maidenhead College of Further Education for all their help and for lending me their work to photograph. Also my thanks to Jan Messent for her advice and for the drawings she did for me, to my daughter Sarah for her drawings, to my daughter Louise for taking on the housekeeping so that I could write the text, and to everyone who so kindly let me take photographs of their designs and embroideries.

Valerie Harding

Newbury, Berkshire 1979

Introduction

Man has always been fascinated by the human form and has expressed this fascination in many different ways. Faces and figures have been drawn, painted, sculpted, carved, embroidered and depicted in other media for many centuries in a more or less realistic manner usually to tell a story, either real or legendary, or to show a way of life.

In a composition the eye will be drawn first to a face or a figure, so the use of either will create a natural focal point even when combined with a landscape, an interior or with other subjects such as animals.

Those of us who do not draw people from life are wary of tackling this subject and there is much apprehension among embroiderers when they try to use figures in a design. There are ways of designing them which can be more suitable to many embroidery methods than drawing and this book will suggest some which will be shown to be successful. Sometimes the simpler designs which are stylised are more easily interpreted in threads and fabrics and leave more scope for the imagination.

It is worth studying the ways that faces and figures have been treated by artists and craftsmen from other periods and countries to glean ideas from their methods and to adapt them to embroidery. Sometimes figures have been used in a realistic way, sometimes in a purely decorative fashion and sometimes in a highly symbolic one. All approaches are valid depending on the ultimate purpose of the embroidery.

It is also worth considering the more intellectual aspect of man and his environment as subjects for pictures and panels, and projects such as man bound by convention, man triumphant, man engulfed, man being dominated by his environment, man at work or play, or man and machinery, can be studied at depth and will result in some really thoughtful pieces of work.

Historical investigation

Embroideries from all over the world and from other times can suggest many approaches to the design of faces and figures and many different ways of carrying out the design. Close study of the actual pieces is the most satisfactory way and more information can be extracted by this method than by looking at books. However, this is not always possible and a good photograph is better than nothing. Embroideries which can be handled so that one can look at the back as well as the front, and embroideries which are beginning to wear away are always interesting as one can see, for example, how the design was put onto the fabric, or exactly what was used for the padding of a certain area.

Embroideries of faces and figures can be very roughly divided into categories according to the methods used and when studied the minor variations often suggest ways in which our designs can be interpreted.

Appliqué

Appliqué is the sewing of smaller pieces of fabric to a ground fabric so that they form a pattern. It is quicker than stitchery and the results are usually bolder and rely mainly on colour for effect. It is probably one of the earliest forms of decoration and evolved from patching a hole. It has been used all over the world. Sometimes there is no further decoration and sometimes stitchery is added to cover the raw edges or add emphasis to the design. The edges can be turned in and hemmed to stop them fraying.

In the middle ages in Europe applied work was used as an economical substitute for embroidery and at a later period it reproduced the effect of the expensive woven fabrics.

In Iran felt is found applied to wool, and in England velvet to wool or silk. Other fabrics such as leather, cloth of gold or silk have been used. In the Burmese wall hangings, known as Kalangas, cotton is applied to cotton or velvet. These hangings are pictorial with figures and other motifs and the themes are either secular or religious. In Nigeria the men work battle scenes on wall hangings with figures applied in red, green or blue cotton to a black (usually) cotton ground.

Another use for appliqué was the sewing of motifs which have been embroidered on a different fabric to a silk or velvet ground. This was done partly because of the difficulty of working on a fabric

1 A figure from the story of Tristram on a hanging. Appliqué outlined with cord. Germany fifteenth century

2 Figures from the Bible quilt made in 1886 by Harriet Powers of Georgia, USA. Stories are told beginning with Adam and Eve and ending with the Birth of Christ. Cotton pieces are applied to cotton

9

3 A Kuna Indian mola with a marauding mermaid design. The detail shows the cut, turned and hemmed shapes that are so characteristic of this work and are represented by lines in the main drawing. The colours are red, orange, green and yellow

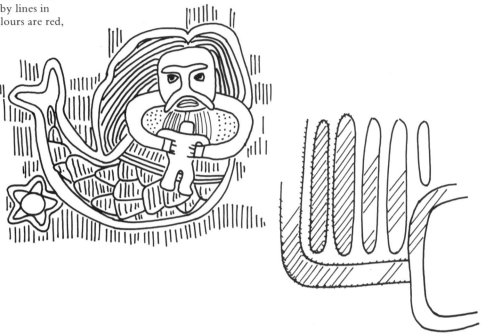

such as velvet and partly because more than one person worked the motifs for a single embroidery. This technique was used extensively during medieval times in Europe, and again in England in the sixteenth century when figures and other motifs were often worked in cross or tent stitch on linen were applied to white satin.

The Kuna Indians have a method of appliqué in which two or more layers of cotton are tacked together and progressively smaller shapes are cut out of each layer to show the different colours. The edges are hemmed and sometimes more shapes are applied.

Outlines

A method of embroidering figures often used was to stitch around the outline, usually with a medium or dark toned thread on a pale background. Sometimes details were added within the outlines. Open fillings were used on certain pieces and the backgrounds were either left untreated or filled in with a simple stitch such as running or seeding. The ground stitching was carried out in a thread that was either the same or paler than the fabric. The outline stitch was usually back stitch as it gives a definite line and is easy to manoeuvre around intricate details, but chain or stem were also used. In India chain stitch was often worked with a tambour hook and this technique was also used in France, China and other parts of Asia. The stitching can quilt two or three layers together thus serving more than one purpose.

4 A copy of part of the Guicciardini quilt showing Tristram. Back stitch in brown thread and running stitch in ecru on linen. Sicily 1400

5 A head worked in white chain stitch on white linen with a drawn ground. Saxony mid-thirteenth century

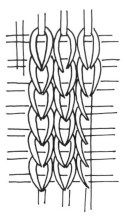

6 Knitting stitch

Worked backgrounds

An approach used a great deal in Europe at different periods was to embroider the background of the design in a single stitch leaving the shapes unworked or with only the barest detail indicated.

Drawn ground   Pairs of threads were withdrawn from linen in both directions and the remaining pairs were worked as shown in the diagram. This technique was used in Germany in the thirteenth century, in England in the fourteenth century and in Sicily in the eighteenth century as a background for figures, sometimes with birds and animals and plants. Usually the stitching was worked in white on white.

Long-legged cross stitch   This was used a great deal in Italy in the sixteenth and seventeenth centuries using red or green silk on natural linen. Examples are also found in Morocco and Czechoslovakia of figures with plants treated in this way. The background was totally covered by the stitching to make the figures stand out well.

Knitting stitch   There is an example of this on a fourteenth century German panel in London showing the Adoration of the Kings. The background is totally covered in green with the figures left in the white linen. One or two details such as eyes and hair are worked in brick stitch.

Other stitches used to cover the ground were french knots and eyelets.

12

7 Part of a white linen border with figures, animals and birds, on a drawn ground. Sicily eighteenth century

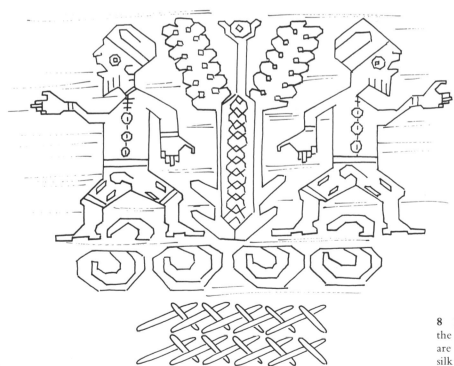

8 Long-armed cross stitch filling in the background to the motifs which are outlined in double-running. Red silk on linen. Italy sixteenth century

13

9 Two figures from the Bayeux tapestry which tells the story of the Norman conquest of England. Wool is laid in rows and details are couched on top. England 1080

10 An ancient Peruvian embroidery showing a hunter holding the shrunken head of an enemy, worked in stem stitch

Using one stitch only

There are many examples of embroideries of figures worked in a single stitch to totally or partially fill the shapes and sometimes the background as well. Stem stitch was used in China, Peru and Chile. Running stitch was used in Sweden in vertical rows to fill stylised figure shapes. In Italy in the sixteenth and seventeenth centuries borders were worked mainly in red silk on linen, but sometimes in brown, using double running or Holbein stitch. In the Greek Islands in the eighteenth century double running and double darning in coloured silks filled in figures with birds or boats and also in Norway in the thirteenth century. Loop stitch was used in Ancient Peru and was worked in parallel rows with wools of different colours. An interesting use of square eyelets is found in Iceland where they totally fill in both the design and the background in subtly coloured wool threads on linen.

14

11 Detail of a border worked in back
stitch in brown on linen. Italy sixteenth
century
Victoria and Albert Museum, London

12 Russian peasant motif worked in double running

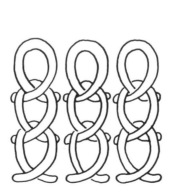

13 Loop stitch which is worked from the bottom up. This stitch was used in ancient Peru to fill figure shapes in wool on cotton fabric

14 A solid filling of eyelets in different colours was used in traditional Icelandic embroideries to cover the design and the background

Cretan stitch Many embroideries from Crete used this stitch as a thick line and also to fill small shapes, usually in red, yellow and blue. Sirens, mermaids and figures with urns and plants were popular subjects.

17

16 Detail of a panel worked in tent stitch in silk on linen canvas which tells of the finding of Moses. Britain early seventeenth century.
The Embroiderers' Guild, London

Tent stitch This was used a great deal in England in the sixteenth, seventeenth and eighteenth centuries using silk and wool on linen. Various colours were used with shading to indicate form. Biblical and pastoral scenes and portraits were worked on pole screens, pictures, boxes, table carpets, cushions and bags. It was also much used in Germany in the sixteenth century.

18

17 An Indian figure worked in chain stitch in red, yellow and orange with black outlines

18 Detail of a bedspread in white cotton embroidered with yellow silk in chain stitch. Indo-Portuguese early seventeenth century
Victoria and Albert Museum, London

Chain stitch This stitch was often worked as a solid filling following the outline of the shape to be filled and gradually nearing the centre. In Iraq it was worked on wall hangings and rugs, and also in India. There are examples of English embroideries worked in this way, in particular an eighteenth century coverlet with little figures with bows and arrows using red and brown chain stitch in silk on linen.

19

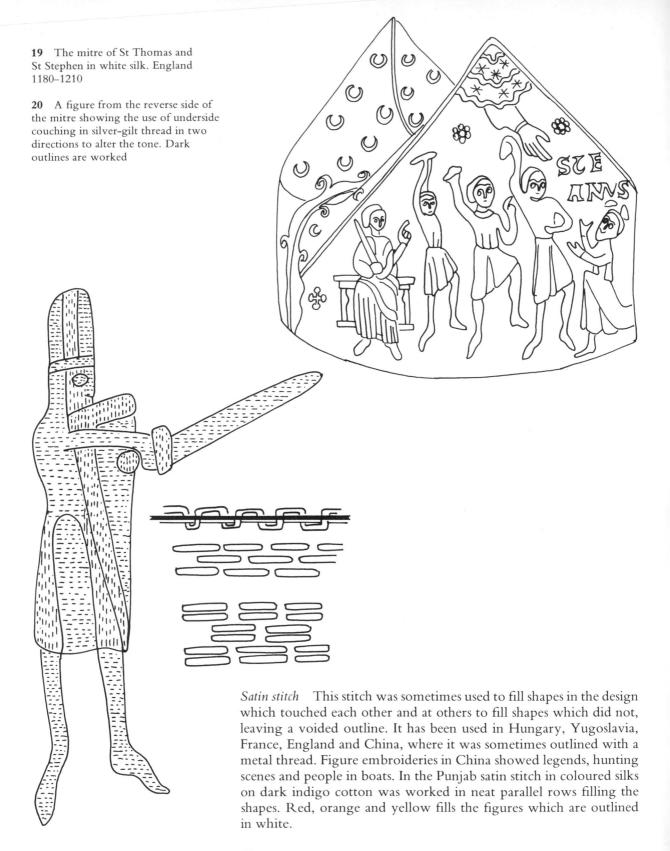

19 The mitre of St Thomas and St Stephen in white silk. England 1180–1210

20 A figure from the reverse side of the mitre showing the use of underside couching in silver-gilt thread in two directions to alter the tone. Dark outlines are worked

Satin stitch   This stitch was sometimes used to fill shapes in the design which touched each other and at others to fill shapes which did not, leaving a voided outline. It has been used in Hungary, Yugoslavia, France, England and China, where it was sometimes outlined with a metal thread. Figure embroideries in China showed legends, hunting scenes and people in boats. In the Punjab satin stitch in coloured silks on dark indigo cotton was worked in neat parallel rows filling the shapes. Red, orange and yellow fills the figures which are outlined in white.

20

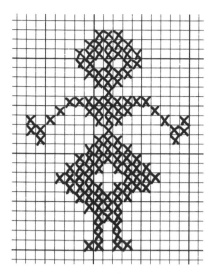

21 A cross stitch figure from a small embroidered rag made by a Huichol Indian which was attached to an arrow and left to rot. It represents a prayer for the health of a person

22 A cross stitch figure from an Icelandic wall hanging in wool showing the use of voided lines

23 Figures filled in with pattern darning in black and mid-brown wool on linen. Iceland

Long and short stitch This has been used in England, Japan, seventeenth century Italy where it was combined with couched metal threads, and in eighteenth century Germany.

Cross stitch This is another widely used stitch and is found in Japan, North Africa, the Eastern Mediterranean and all over Europe and Scandinavia. Sometimes the whole design is carried out in one colour and sometimes in many colours. It is usually worked on white, cream or natural linen.

Pattern darning This method was used in Russia, Greece, Japan, East Africa, Indonesia, Ancient Peru and Central America where it was worked in horizontal rows to fill in the shapes, leaving the ground unworked.

21

24 A head solidly filled in with blue, black and yellow beads on a plain ground. Egypt first century

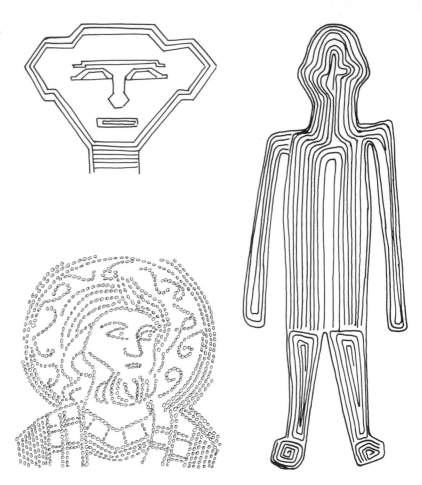

25 A panel of a stole using coral, gold and blue glass beads and seed pearls sewn to parchment. Germany thirteenth century

26 Figure from Powhattan's mantle filled in with shells sewn to leather along the lines indicated. Virginia, USA. early seventeenth century

27 Chinese knot

Using beads or knots

Beads or knots were used to partially or totally fill the shapes in a design, sometimes alone or with a couched thread or stitched outlines. Different coloured beads made the design easier to read. This method is found in Egypt, Greece, Germany, England, and among the north and South American Indians.

In China many embroideries were carried out using the Chinese, or Peking, knot which filled large areas in regular rows in shades of a colour. This was often outlined with a couched thread.

28 Detail from St Cuthbert's maniple showing Peter the Deacon. The figure is embroidered in stem and split stitch in coloured silk, and the background is underside couching in silver-gilt thread. England 909–916

Using more than one stitch

A great many embroideries were worked using more than one stitch, sometimes more than one method. The background was sometimes left untreated but more often is part of the design as a whole. The faces and hands were usually stitched but occasionally were painted, often when the scale of the design was too small to allow for stitching the features.

29 St Thomas from the Syon cope.
Split stitch in coloured silk on linen
with the background of underside
couching. England late thirteenth
century
Victoria and Albert Museum, London

One of the most important periods in English embroidery is known as *Opus Anglicanum* and took place between about 1250 and 1350. The embroideries were worked by professional craftsmen although the designs were first drawn on the fabric by painters. The subjects were Ecclesiastical and largely figurative and were used as a method of

30 Melchior's head from the Bamberg altar frontal, The crown and robe are couched silver–gilt, and all else is worked in chain stitch in vertical rows. The colour changes at the outlines. Germany 1300

teaching, so the figures were identified by their symbols. Saints were a popular theme and also angels. The figures are short with disproportionately large hands and feet, and the eyes enlarged to give them importance. Sometimes the most important figure in the design is enlarged for the same reason. The poses and gestures are very expressive. The designs are stylised and the shape of the figure was planned in relation to the shape it filled.

The heads hands and feet were usually worked in split stitch in coloured silk with the direction of the stitching emphasising the form of the face. The cheeks were often worked in a spiral, but an alternative method was to work vertical rows of stitching to fill the face and neck and to outline the features afterwards. The hair was often worked in alternated light and dark rows of split stitch. Shading gave form to the body and garments and the stitching followed the line of the limbs and the folds of the robes. The backgrounds were often worked in underside couching in silver gilt making intricate patterns. Other stitches used at this period were satin, knots, stem, cross, tent and plaited stitch. Figures were embroidered on copes, chasubles, orphreys and panels, some of which were cut up at a later date to alter their shape or to make into other articles.

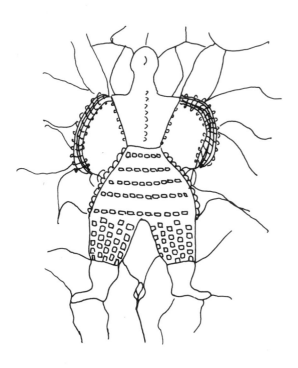

31 A detail from a chalice cover in needlepoint lace using buttonhole stitch. Italy sixteenth century

32 A figure from a stumpwork casket. The face and hands are padded, with satin stitch around the eyes and across the hands. The dress is made of detached buttonhole shapes applied over padding, and the collar and cuffs are the same but finer. The pieces are not attached at the bottom edge. Green, fawn and red on white satin. England 1660

Buttonhole stitch   This stitch in its different forms has been a popular one in many countries, usually combined with other stitches. In the Philippines very fine embroidery was worked using a white silk thread on fine white cotton, including buttonhole and satin stitches with pulled thread fillings. In England in the seventeenth century it was used with tent stitch and the figures were applied to white satin. In Germany in the fourteenth century it combined with chain and split stitch to fill in whole shapes using white thread on white linen. The outlines were left as gaps in the stitching. Buttonhole in its detached form was used in sixteenth century Switzerland with couching and overcast herringbone in coloured silks on linen. In England in the middle of the seventeenth century detached buttonhole was used a great deal, with other stitches, on pictures, boxes, and mirror frames in Biblical, mythical or woodland scenes with figures, animals and plants. A special version was used for collars, cuffs, skirts, bodices and capes on these little figures as well as for curtains, leaves and flower petals. To work this version a row of stitches was sewn around the edge of a shape and detached buttonhole was worked into the stitches only, not going through the fabric. When the shape was filled the preliminary stitches were cut away from most of the outline leaving the buttonhole shape free except at one edge.

26

33 An embroidered casket with a
miniature garden inside the lid. White
satin with coloured silks and metal
thread. England 1650–1675
Victoria and Albert Museum, London

34 A detail from a hanging of St Joseph (in contemporary dress) with buildings and fields. Stem, back and straight stitches on linen. England seventeenth century

Flat stitches Stem and satin stitch were popular in many countries at different periods, either in wool or silk. Sometimes many colours were used in the same piece and at others only one colour was used which could be the same as the background. These stitches completely filled in the faces and figures, with details in other stitches, and sometimes an outline around the edge in stem, back stitch or couching. In England in the middle of the seventeenth century there was a vogue for embroidery in one colour, often in black, red or blue, worked on linen using stem, running, back stitch and seeding. This was very practical and could be laundered.

35 Part of an infant's gown made of
lawn, embroidered but never made up.
Satin, seeding, trailing, eyelets, ladder
stitch and spiders' webs on a pulled
work ground. Portugal nineteenth
century
The Embroiderers' Guild, London

36 *Sursum Corda* a panel using darning and stitchery in wools on an evenly woven fabric by Dorothy Angus, made in the 1920s

Metal thread work

In Britain and on the Continent of Europe from the fourteenth century onwards much rich embroidery was worked using silver and silver-gilt thread, purls, spangles and coloured silks. Often the gilt thread was couched over card or leather shapes to make a hard raised area, and also over padding or string. There is an English pulpit fall of the seventeenth century which has all these techniques showing angels' heads with each chin resting on a pair of wings. The whole is very highly raised and padded on a background of purple velvet.

Some of the methods described were used in other places and are still in use in some countries. There is so much to study in the embroideries of the past that one can get very confused and the trick is to isolate one particular method or stitch and play about with it, adapting it to your own design, rather than get bogged down with looking at too much at once.

37 Part of a white organdie runner with the fabric double in some places. Satin, Seeding, buttonhole, pulled work, eyelets, shadow work, darning and whipped running stitch. Italy 1948 The Embroiderers' Guild, London

Sources of design

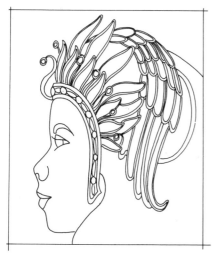

38 Theatrical head-dress of a dancer made of gold leather and gold berries. The leaves are slightly padded and stand away from the head

Ideas for designs can come from many other arts and crafts and drawings or photographs of them can be traced and re-traced, altered and adapted until your design is completed. It is worth looking at the way other races at different periods have solved the problem of portraying the human figure in various media as one can learn much from studying these sources. Painting, sculpture, mosaics, stained glass windows, old pattern books, textiles, posters, brass rubbings and other crafts are a rich source of material for a designer. One can study them for different qualities such as the proportions of the various parts of the body, facial expressions, how the folds of the drapery have been portrayed, the positions of the limbs, hairstyles, how the figure has been stylised or abstracted, or how it has been designed to fit the position it occupies. The human figure has fascinated all races at every period of time and has been depicted in hundreds of ways, so much so that one wonders if anything new can be thought of, but it always can. Even if two people used the same source material the results would be quite different because their methods of adaption would be different. One can start by keeping a file of cuttings taken from magazines, postcards from museums, one's own photographs, and photocopies of designs from books and sketches. It will be a life-time's study but will always be interesting.

39 A clay model of the demon Humbaba from Assyria, seventh century BC

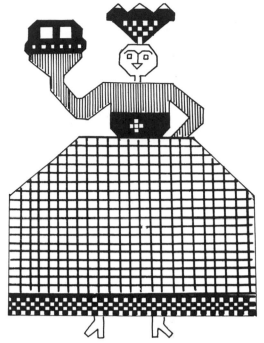

Top left **40** A gorgoneion, painted on an
Athenian plate. Sixth century BC

41 Russian peasant design from a
book published in 1872

42 Drawing by Jan Messent of the
mosaic head of the Empress Theodora
from San Vitale, Ravenna, Italy,
Circa AD 547

43 Drawing by Joan Hake of a fourth century Sassanian King's head

44 Embroidery by Joan Hake worked on red cheesecloth using purple and mustard leather, navy net, needle-weaving, couching, buttonhole loops, plaiting and braid stitch. Parts are padded

45 A head from a painting by Salvador Dali, obviously based on a Roman statue. The landscape background shows through the face between the shaded areas

Paintings

This is a most fruitful source of inspiration as some of the greatest artists have considered that painting people was the most difficult but interesting thing to do. People have been painted realistically, in a very stylised way and as total abstraction of the various parts of the human form. A more stylised painting or one painted in a technique such as pointillism is often more useful to the embroiderer than a realistic one. Van Gogh's brush strokes, for example, suggest groups of stitches, small pieces of fabric laid on a background to build up the picture and machined over, or a use of the reverse appliqué of the Kuna Indians. This is impossible to draw in black and white as the whole effect depends on different colours being used.

36

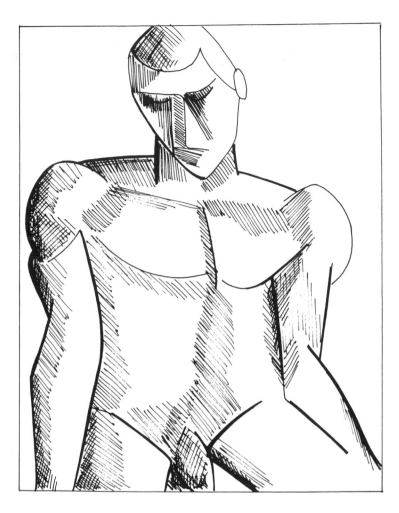

46 A figure from a painting by Picasso which suggests strength, solidity and masculinity

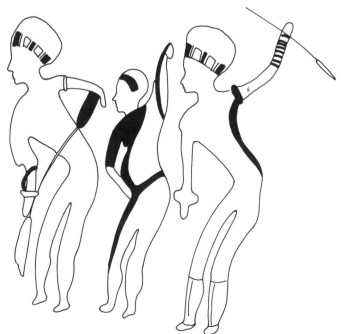

47 Cave painting of hunters from Tassili in the Sahara desert. 5000 BC

48 Drawing by Sheila Kinross of a basalt head of the Storm God of the Hitites

49 Blackwork embroidery by Sheila Kinross adapted from the drawing using wine thread on white scrim

50 Head of an archer, taken from a carving on the Tripylon Staircase at Persepolis. The embroidery by Sheila Kinross is worked on canvas using tent, cushion, mosaic, leaf, Hungarian, Algerian eye and fishbone stitches

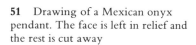

51 Drawing of a Mexican onyx
pendant. The face is left in relief and
the rest is cut away

52 Celtic stonework

Sculptures

As sculpture and stone carvings are fairly indestructible there is plenty
of material available for study. Sometimes one's own city has a
particularly interesting cathedral or college building or gravestone
in the churchyard that can be photographed easily. It may be necessary
to use a telephoto lense on the camera but at least the statues or gargoyles are not inside a glass case, and often one can see different views
of the object and greater information can be gleaned from it. Drawing
does take more time than photography but is more selective. Really
one needs both approaches for the different qualities they offer. Bas-
reliefs are useful as they can be translated into quilted or padded
designs, or the tonal variations caused by the light striking them from
one direction can be useful when designing for blackwork.

53 'African Double Mask' based on a wood carving. The faces are highly padded felt. They were seamed down the centre to get the curved shape with the noses and mouths added afterwards. Some canvas work, leather, tweed and velvet in the head-dress
Embroidery by Jan Messent, reproduced by courtesy of Mrs N. Fletcher

54 A three-dimensional African head, carved in wood and highly polished, The angle of the face is interesting and the way the neck is enlarged to make a firm base

55 Stone Virgin and Child from Liverpool Cathedral. The treatment of the garments suggests pleated and folded fabric over a padded shape

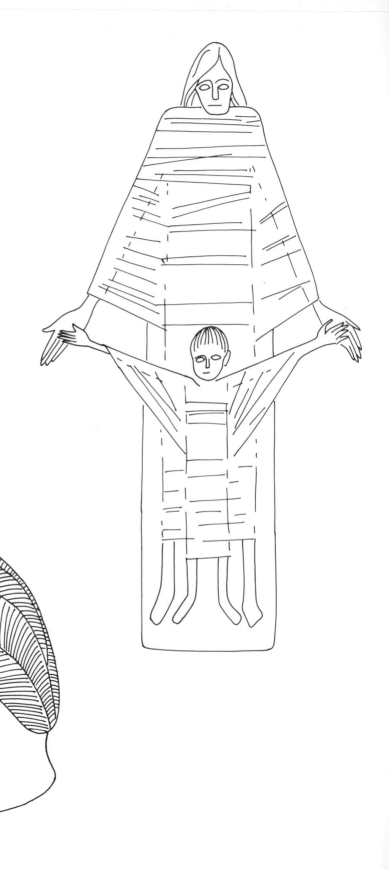

56 Painting of a bas-relief from
Mexico. AD 700

57 Motifs from textiles. (a) Chimu warrior from Peru. Fourteenth century. (b) An Indonesian figure in which details such as teeth and ribs are used as pattern to break up the large areas. (c) Ancestor figure from the Phillipines. Nineteenth century

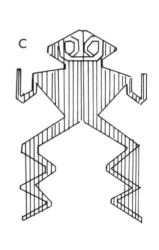

A

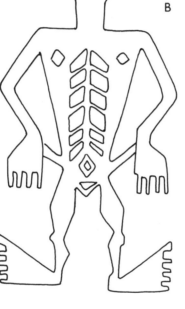

B

C

Textiles

Woven rugs, blankets and wall hangings often incorporate figures into the design and the technique of necessity has stylised the shapes even if the designer has set out to be realistic, which he or she usually has not. The manner of stylisation is in tune with the style of that period and country, but the weaving has super-imposed its own discipline. Designs from textiles are particularly suited to counted thread methods of embroidery.

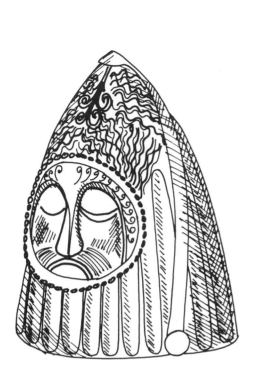

58 Drawing of a chessman made by Malcolm Appleby of steel, gold and silver

59 Gold amulet from the Ivory Coast. The face is in relief and the decoration around it of wire

Metal work

Bronzes, jewellery, household articles such as jugs or platters with embossed faces or figures as decoration, and treasures of gold or silver are usually treated in a decorative manner that can suggest an embroidery method. Embossing suggests padding, piercing suggests cutwork, and enamelling on gold suggests using coloured stitching with the gold embroidery. The difficulty with these articles is that they are so decorative in themselves that it is tempting to use them just as they are whereas it is vital to adapt and alter them. Extract the elements in the design that appeal to you, leave out the others, add other shapes, lines or spaces that contribute to your design which should only be based on the original, not a copy of it.

60 The bronze Sanctuary door knocker from Durham Cathedral

45

61 Helmet from a suit of Japanese armour
Victoria and Albert Museum, London

62 Embroidery by Brough Atkinson based on the Sutton Hoo mask. Gold kid, purls, sequins, bronze and blue-green beads and gold threads on green fabric

63 Greek masks by Mollie Taylor based on ancient theatrical masks. Padding, applied pieces of leather, wooden beads, chain stitch and couching in cream, fawn, green and rust

64 German executioner's mask made of velvet and laminated paper

Masks

Masks can be beautiful, awe-inspiring or frightening depending on the intention. A mask confers on the wearer a special personality, prestige, disguise or protection. Usually it is worn over the face but can cover the body as well. Man has used masks for over 15 000 years mainly for theatrical or religious uses, and these are the most interesting ones. They have been made of many substances such as wood, straw, papier mâché, metal or rope. In some civilizations masks were thought to confer eternal youthfulness on the dead, and were made particularly splendid. A mask can be held in front of the face by a rod or handle, it can sit on top of the head and hang down over the face, or it can be supported by the shoulders.

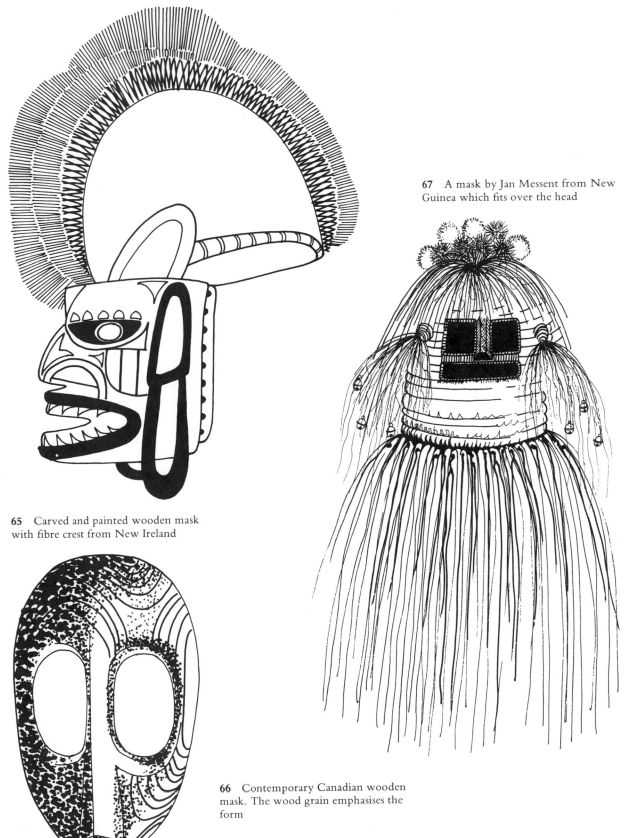

67 A mask by Jan Messent from New Guinea which fits over the head

65 Carved and painted wooden mask with fibre crest from New Ireland

66 Contemporary Canadian wooden mask. The wood grain emphasises the form

68 Detail of the mask by Jean Mould
shown in colour plate facing page 96
showing the metal thread textures

Photographs

To take photographs of other people in interesting situations is not always easy. One's family usually refuse and other people are often self-conscious. However, a candid shot of strangers in the street, or a person concentrating on something so much that they do not realise what is happening is possible. The high standard of photography today means that we are flooded with material in books, magazines and newspapers and there is plenty of variety available provided one bothers to collect and file it. As an alternative to real people, artists' wooden models, 'Action Man' or dolls can be used. One can always photograph oneself in a mirror, using a delayed action device, or by pointing the camera at one's feet.

It is possible to take photographs of a television screen if you set your camera at $\frac{1}{30}$ second and the aperture at f5.6 or f4. Although the picture will not be of very high quality it will be a record that will spark off the imagination. Medical photographs such as X-rays, heat-maps of areas of the body and photographs taken through a micro-scope are beyond the capabilities of most of us, but reproductions of these are often to be found in books or magazines.

69 Photograph of a wig stand inside a pair of black tights. The distortion of the net as it expands and contracts around the shape of the head changes the tone value in places

51

70 Three girls dancing. Photography used for capturing an 'instant of time'

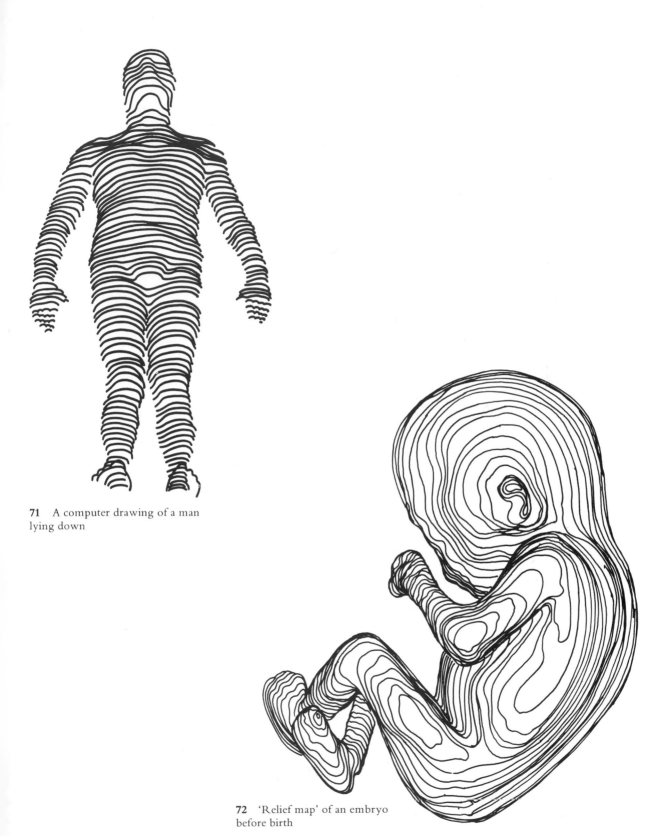

71 A computer drawing of a man lying down

72 'Relief map' of an embryo before birth

53

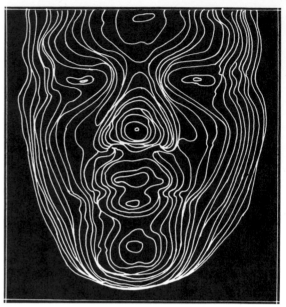

73 Scraperboard version of a contour map of a face

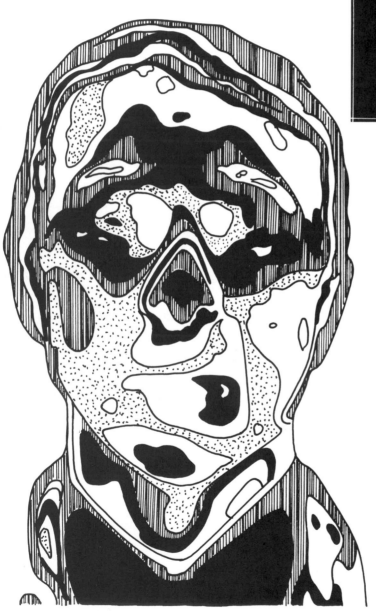

74 Heat map of a man's head

Proportion and distortion

Proportion

Artists usually try to grasp the essence of the form of the body and the movement that it is capable of. We should understand the skeleton, the muscle action and the correct proportions of the heads, limbs and trunk to be able to use the figure in a design. If the shapes are distorted it must be for a reason and not because of lack of understanding.

Photographs and quick sketches of people in different positions can be collected for reference and traced for using in a design. Beware of using the card figure models with connections at the joints as it is only too easy to place them in positions that the body is not capable of assuming. A wooden three-dimensional artist's model can be used instead.

75 The muscles of the back

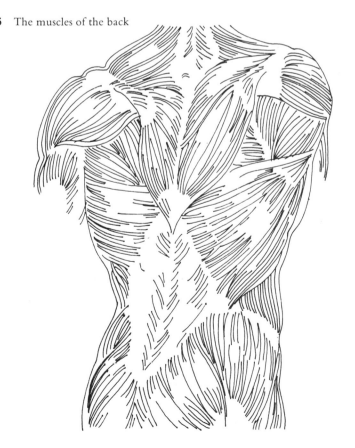

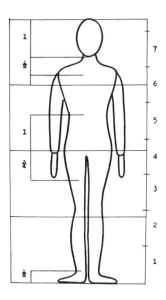

76 The correct proportions of the figure. The lines right across divide the figure into quarters and the numbers refer to the parts measured in terms of heads

The figure can be divided into parts based on the measurement of the head from the top of the skull to the chin. The whole equals 7.5 or 8 heads, the back equals 2 heads, a leg 3.5 heads, the width across the shoulders 2 heads and the length of the hand 1 head. Of course people vary slightly, particularly in the length of their legs, but this is a rough guide.

There has been a great deal of variety in the shape and proportion of the face and skull during the process of evolution from primitive man to the present day. Early man had similarities to the ape with a ridge above the eyes which strengthened the brow and a very strong prominent jaw. Gradually the jaw receded and the face became more vertical and the skull enlarged to allow more room for the brain. At the same time the arms became shorter, the legs longer and the posture more upright. A baby has a much larger forehead and cranium than an adult and a shorter distance from eye to mouth. The head of a newborn baby is one fifth of its total length, and female heads are usually smaller than male in proportion to their length. Children's proportions alter gradually during the growing period, remembering that the younger the child the faster the growth rate. Adults are usually slightly stockier than teenagers.

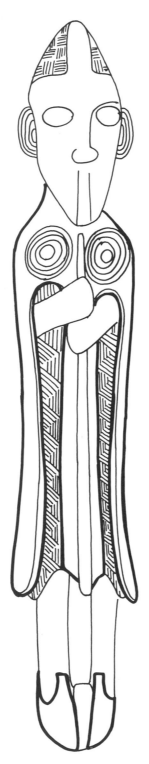

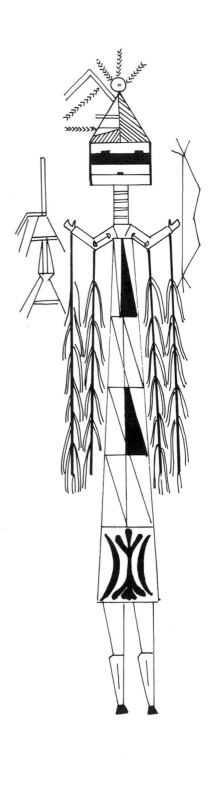

77 A bronze figure of a Bishop showing differential distortion. Ireland twelfth century

78 A Navajo sand painting made for a religious ceremony showing the very elongated body and shortened limbs

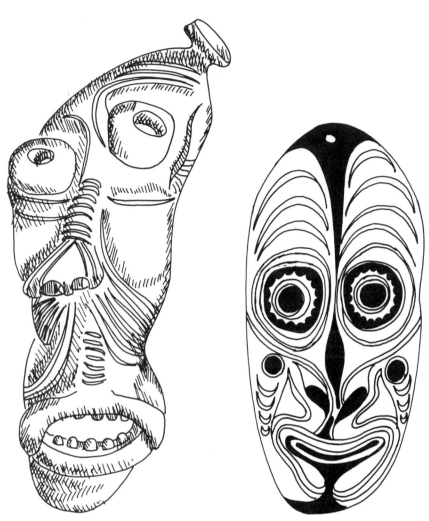

79 Gross distortion of the face in this African carving which is powerful but unpleasant

80 Stylised distortion in this carved and painted wooden gable end mask from the Sepik area of New Guinea

81 A Peruvian fifteenth century gold ornament which shows a face designed to fit a rectangle

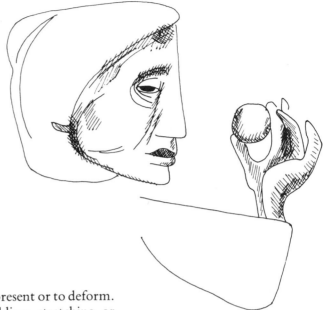

Distortion

This means to pull or twist out of shape, to misrepresent or to deform. It can be achieved by bending, pleating or folding, stretching or shrinking, splitting or cracking. It can also be due to a change in the position of the viewer, or to a reflection in a curved or textured surface. Photographic distortion can be obtained by several methods including photographing a person with a wide-angle lens from close to.

We are so accustomed to slight distortion, such as in fashion drawing when the figure is elongated for the sake of elegance, that we tend not to notice it until it becomes exaggerated. A face is distorted by force such as a strong wind, gravity or a blow, or when it is pressed against a window or seen through textured glass.

The purposes of distortion are to indicate character or personality; to indicate ideas, feelings or emotions; for emphasis; to indicate importance; or for the sake of the composition and to fit a particular space. The baser side of man is as valid a subject as the heroic side and the statement you wish to make is not always pleasant. Ugliness has dramatic impact and distortion adds to this drama.

Both primitive and modern art make use of distortion but in different manners and for different reasons. Primitive artists were not interested in portraying individuals and used distortion because of their style of art, because of the limitation of the medium they were working in, for the emphasis of certain characteristics, for the sake of symbolism, or for the projection of ideas which were usually religious in the broadest sense.

82 Woman from a painting by Robert Colquhoun. Slight distortion and stylisation to indicate character and personality

59

83 *Grandad Dozing* A panel by Olive James with applied fabrics, shading using nets, stuffed areas, knots and couched threads. The folded and padded fabric of the face indicates age and relaxation

Modern artists use distortion to further the accurate portrayal of reality as they see it and to extract the essence of the object that is being portrayed. They also use it because of the demands of the medium or for the sake of stylisation.

Alteration of the viewpoint

If one is looking at a person or their face or parts of their body from above or below, foreshortening takes place which alters the apparent lengths of the various parts. A photograph can be held at different angles to achieve a similar effect, but as the photograph is on a single plane the results will be different. More than one viewpoint can be combined in the same design as did the ancient Egyptians when they used the front view for some parts of the body and the side view for others.

84 A basketwork figure from the Pima Indians of Arizona showing stylisation demanded by the medium

Distortion through stylisation

This is often practised when designing and parts of the face and body are reduced to simplified or geometric shapes. Sometimes this is done for the sake of simplification and sometimes because the medium demands it. It is often necessary for embroidery and the method used to carry out the design often determines the type of stylisation. A counted thread technique will not allow smooth curves so the design must be built up of straight lines, however short.

Shadows and reflections

When someone is reflected in a curved surface such as a silver meat cover, a car hub cap or a Christmas tree ball, or when a shadow is cast onto a shaped surface, distortion will result. This can often be very interesting and worth noting. An extension of this is the projection of a transparency (or a negative in a transparency holder) onto shaped objects such as bowls or boxes. If the object is covered with paper, the design can be drawn while it is being projected.

Transparent media

When looking through water, textured glass, a bottle, a glass brick, crumpled cellophane or a magnifying glass, the person being viewed is distorted. Try and photograph this if possible as it is difficult to hold something with one hand while drawing with the other, or there may not be time.

85 Stylised figures from signs

61

86 A photograph of two girls
dancing taken by strobe lighting which
gives more than one exposure on the
same negative. Multiple image
distortion

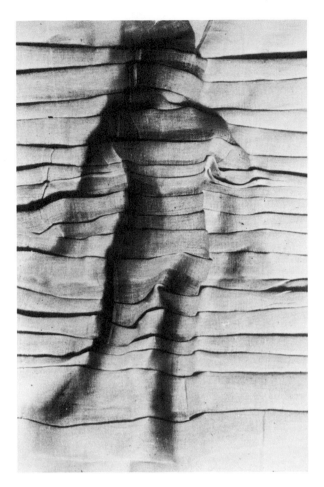

87 A wooden doll whose outlines are blurred and changed by covering it with folded fabric

88 The same doll covered with damp newspaper. The variation in tone of the newsprint distracts the eye from the figure which is difficult to distinguish

89 Drawing by Jean Littlejohn of a Mexican Huastec head and the canvas work based on it. The disc at the back represents the sun's rays. The slight alteration of the proportion is interesting

90 (a) Drawing of a French sailor's clay pipe made in 1750
(b) A grid drawn around the head to divide it into small sections to make re-drawing easier
(c) The design enlarged by re-drawing it within a grid of larger squares
(d) The design widened by altering the horizontal measurement only
(e) The design lengthened by altering the vertical measurement
(f) The design widened at the top
(g) A grid made by drawing along a flexible curve for the vertical lines and straight equally spaced horizontal lines. Drawing the design in this type of grid would lead to a very strange result and is best kept for simple shapes
Grids can be made within circles, ovals and free shapes. A semi-circular grid would be useful for adapting a design for the neckline of a dress

Using grids

The method of enlarging a design by the grid method can lead to the alteration of the shape and proportion of a design so that it will fit into another shape. Enclose the original design in a box and divide it into a particular number of sections by drawing equally spaced lines in both directions. Then draw the proposed change of shape and divide it into the same number of sections. Redraw the design section by section.

64

C

I

D

E

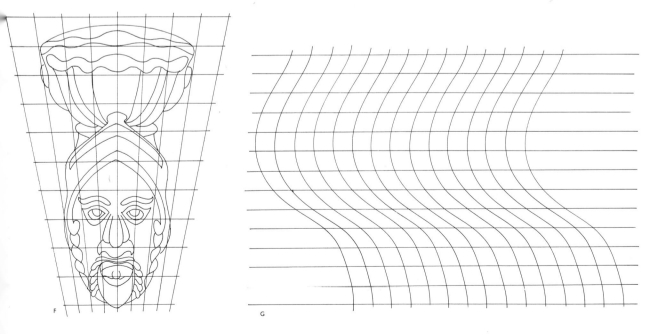

F

G

65

Some design methods

Designing faces and figures can cause apprehension to an embroiderer who thinks that they are very difficult to do. However there are some simple design methods which are perfectly satisfactory provided too much realism is not attempted. A stylised design is easier to carry out in stitchery and more suited to the craft. Faces and figures should be designed to fill the space they are intended to occupy, whether this is the whole area or only a small part of it. For those who prefer not to draw, photography is a very helpful reference tool for designers, and even a simple camera is useful. It can also help with abstraction of shapes by taking high contrast pictures in a strong light which blocks out unwanted detail, or transparencies which are later sandwiched together for multiple images.

Between realism and pure abstraction there are a number of stages. The subject need be only very slightly simplified or can be so abstracted that it is unrecognisable. Slight simplification is probably the most useful stage for embroidery, and a knowledge of the method that is going to be used to carry out the design can be borne in mind when doing the paper work as it suggests how to stylise the figure shapes, but it should not be the dominant factor.

91 Designs based on paintings by Jawlensky in which faces have been reduced to pattern. These would be suitable for canvaswork, patchwork, blackwork or appliqué with solid areas of stitchery

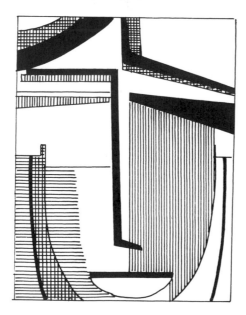

92 (a and b) Two designs by Jenny Bullen taken from the same photograph of a Japanese doll

A

B

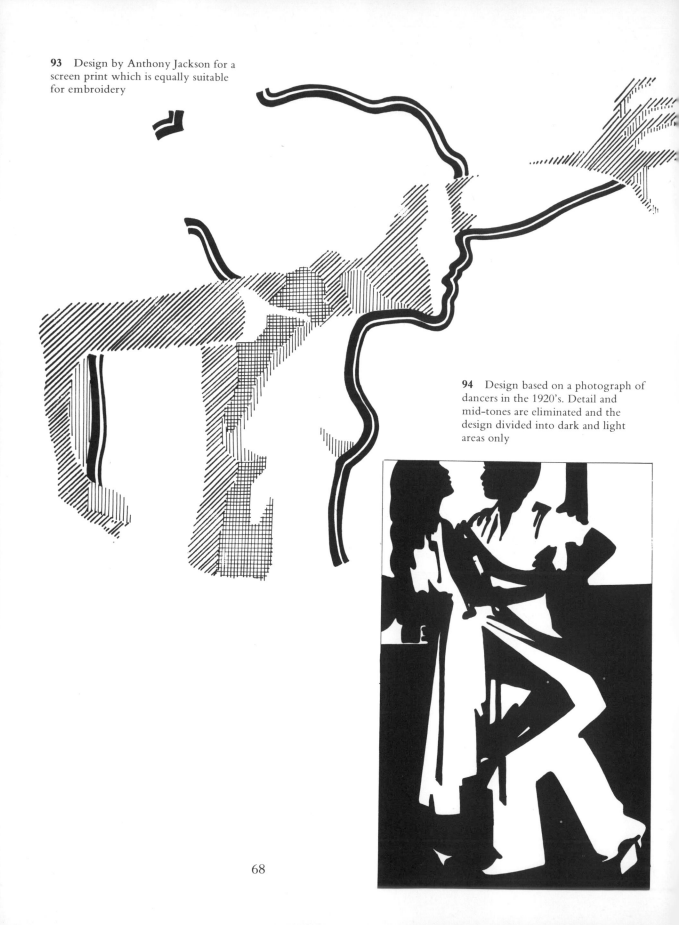

93 Design by Anthony Jackson for a screen print which is equally suitable for embroidery

94 Design based on a photograph of dancers in the 1920's. Detail and mid-tones are eliminated and the design divided into dark and light areas only

95 A detail of the next stage in which the light and dark areas are filled in with torn paper pieces in colours which bear no relation to the original ones, with the tones reversed

96 The embroidery in canvas work
with applied leather. Warm colours
and richer texture are kept to the
centre of the panel and cool colours
and flatter areas to the edges. The wool
used for the embroidery was hand-
spun and dyed using the Russell dye
system
94, 95 and 96 Design and embroidery
by Gisela Banbury, photography by
Pamela Warner

Do not have too much detail in your design. The less distinct is the
thing we look at, the more the imagination supplies and an im-
pressionistic figure gains much from lack of clarity. Also do not draw
the stitchery you are thinking of using as this leads to a too literal
interpretation of the design and leaves no room for development.
Perspective This is a problem that was thought to have no connection
with embroidery, but fashion changes in this respect as in others and
it is now sometimes included in the design. A simple method of
showing that some figures are nearer than others is to make them
larger or place them in front of and overlapping others.

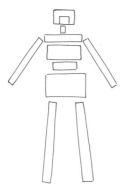

97 A figure built up from rectangles of different sizes and proportions

98 Simple shapes cut from paper which are suitable for appliqué. This is part of a border which could be extended indefinitely and be used on children's clothes, curtains, around a lampshade or on a wall hanging

Colour plate facing
Head by Jan Messent.
Different techniques used together in a colour scheme of creams, naturals and browns with gold. The face is made of felt over card shapes with padded leather and glued string on top. The beard and moustache are machine knitting with macramé over it. Fabric shapes are applied for the hair with some stitchery. See also detail in figure 156

Designing with simple shapes

The face and figure can be reduced to very simple shapes, even geometric ones. Because this idea is simple it is not frightening and can be very successful for many different embroidery methods. Think of mosaics which use squares all of the same size in different colours built up into quite complex designs. Use cut or torn paper pieces and move the shapes about until a satisfactory arrangement is reached and stick them to another sheet of paper. Circles, rectangles or long strips are all good shapes to use as they can be easily translated into rows or blocks of stitches or pieces of fabric. It is more interesting to use different sizes of the same shape to build up the face or figure, and not to use too many different shapes in one design.

Scrap metal shapes such as old curtain rings, nuts and bolts and paper clips can also be used to make a design. Lay these on a piece of paper and then spray paint over them. When it is dry remove the pieces of metal. Another arrangement can be planned on top of the first and then sprayed with a different colour. This method can also be used with fabric and fabric dyes and the embroidery worked by hand or machine afterwards.

Using squared paper

Graph paper or arithmetic books can be used for designing for counted thread embroidery, patchwork, or for embroidery using blocks of stitchery. Isometric graph paper with triangular shapes instead of squares gives interesting results which are particularly suitable for patchwork. Altair paper comes in many different patterns parts of which can be filled in with coloured felt pens. Small designs planned on squared paper tend to be rigid but larger ones allow for more freedom and more interesting results.

72

99 A design on graph paper which is suitable for counted thread embroidery

Colour plate facing
Men and Ladders by Valerie Harding. Card figures covered with felt, satin stitched in coloured threads, and gold threads couched over card shapes with small areas of coloured stitching

100 One of the many Altair sheets filled in to form patterns

73

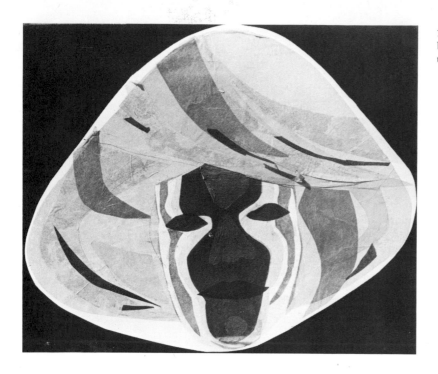

101 Overlapping tissue paper shapes build up this design based on a turbanned head

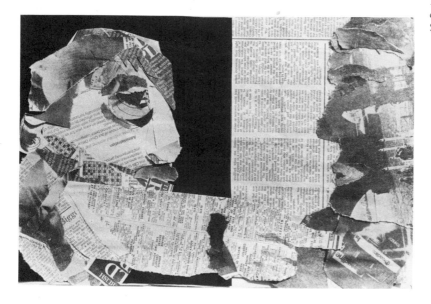

102 Torn newspaper with a few details added in felt pen. Design by Sheila Hill

Cut paper

Using paper shapes to represent pieces of fabric or areas of stitchery is a very useful design method as one can see the areas of tone or colour and the main shapes of the design. They can be stuck to a sheet of card and detail added afterwards with paint or felt pen. If tissue paper is used two colours can overlap to make a third, and if newspaper is used the tones are indicated which is necessary for one colour embroidery such as blackwork.

103 Chinese Tangrams. Divide a square by cutting it along the lines shown in the diagram at the top left. Re-arrange them to form faces or figures not leaving out any of the pieces

104 Design for a King's head based on a 30 cm (12 in.) cube. He could lift up to show a smaller Queen's head, then an even smaller Crown Prince and so on, all fitting inside each other each other like Russian stacking dolls

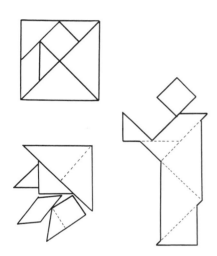

A square piece of card cut as in the Chinese Tangram diagram can produce literally hundreds of faces or figures which, because they are built up using the same shapes, can be put together in the same design. They would be particularly suitable for patchwork or canvas work. Parallel lines of stitchery within the shapes, with different directions in adjacent shapes, would also be a suitable method of interpretation.

When planning a three-dimensional design it is important to do a mock-up in paper or card to decide the shape and proportions. Soft shapes can be made of pinned newspaper pieces stuffed with crumpled newspaper and hard shapes made of pieces of card held together with sticky tape. If the design demands curves or cylinders the card can be held under a running tap until it is damp and then moulded into shape and held with elastic bands until dry when it can be stuck.

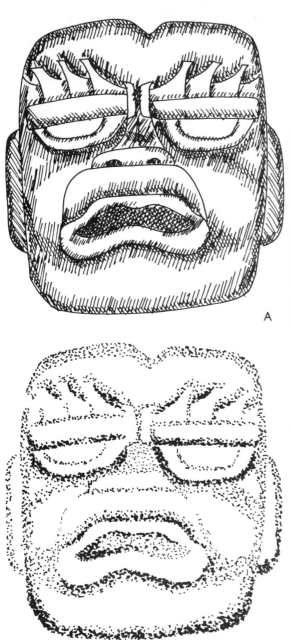

A

B

Designs from books

It is possible to trace designs from pattern books, from books of photographs of other crafts such as sculpture or carving, and from books such as this one. However it is essential to alter and adapt the design, however slightly. The shapes can overlap each other, more lines added, different sizes can be used in one design, or the design cut up and re-arranged, perhaps with certain parts left out. The traced outlines can be laid over another tracing, over a texture or pattern, or

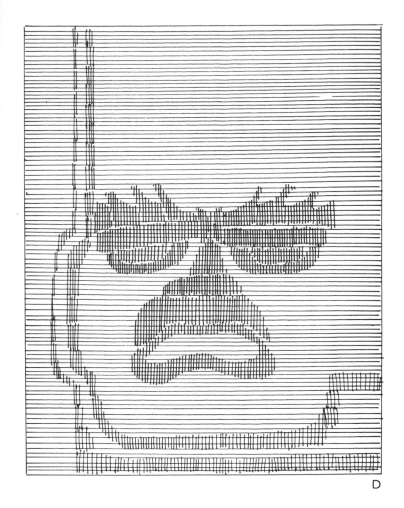

D

105 (a) Drawing of an Olmec carved jade head from a book illustration
(b) A dot drawing of the head which suggests form or relief
(c) A line design based on the original drawing
(d) A further development which could be carried out in Burden stitch. The horizontal lines could be couched threads and the short vertical lines stitches in gold or silk threads, or pieces of purl

over another picture, parts of which are used with the first tracing. For example a tracing of figures can be laid over a picture of a landscape or forest cut from a magazine, and selected parts used to provide a background for the figures. There is no satisfaction in making an exact copy of anything, and if some adaptation happens during the paper work and more at various stages of the embroidery, the end result can be quite unlike the original.

106 (a) Original drawing of a pop
star on tracing paper
(b) The drawing used as a contact
negative for a photographic print with
a projected negative of texture in the
enlarger
(c) A counterchange version

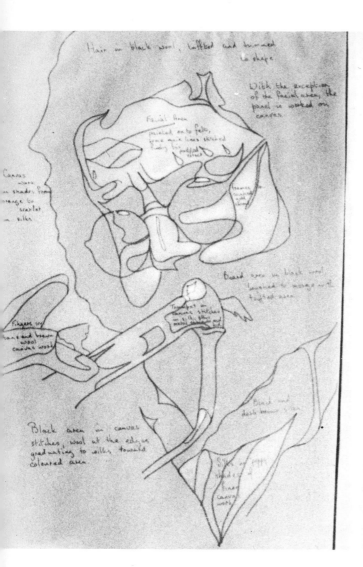

107 *Jazz Man* by Pamela Warner
On the left is a tracing of a photograph
with notes on the proposed colours and
stitches to be used in the embroidery.
On the right is a coloured painting on
paper. The embroidery, which is not
illustrated, is worked in wools on
canvas, with the face in painted and
quilted felt, and tufting for the hair
Photograph by Pamela Warner

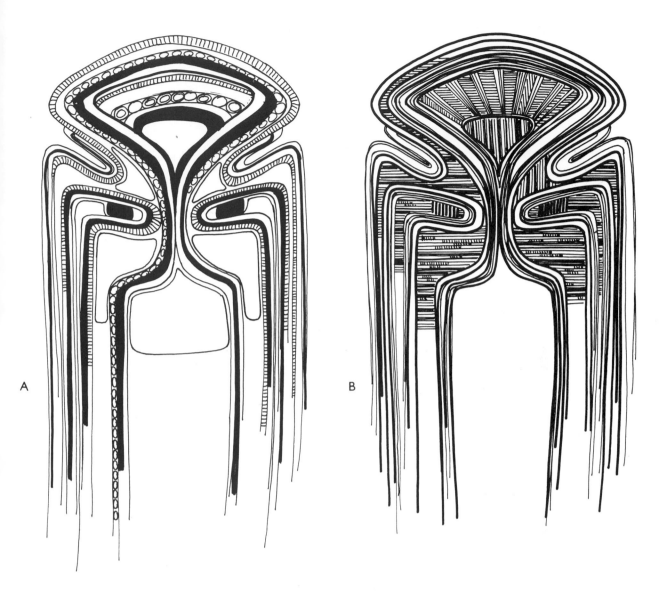

A

B

String designs

Gluing string to a piece of card is time consuming but productive because the result has shape, line and texture and is nearer the final embroidery than some paper designs. Try to combine long and short pieces, different thicknesses, and also different types and colours of string. Manipulating long pieces can be infuriating as they tend to slide about, but some string will stick to sandpaper or velvet long enough for them to be photographed or a rubbing taken. Small pieces of string can be knotted, frayed out, or cut even smaller to add texture, all of which suggests stitchery.

108 (a) A design for a mask which evolved from laying long pieces of string on a piece of sandpaper to stop them flying about and then taking a rubbing. A tracing was made of the rubbing and details added to suggest stitchery and padded areas
(b) Another version of the design in which straight lines contrast with the curved ones

109   String glued to previously
painted card

Drawing

If you can (or will) draw either from life or from your imagination or from articles in museums, there will be much more scope as you can choose unusual points of view, isolate details or include more than one aspect of the original in your drawing. Try to use different media such as biro, felt pen, brush and ink, wax crayon or charcoal. Sometimes these media can be mixed and often fine details can be added with a drawing pen. Blobs or areas of paint can be drawn over and so can pieces of coloured paper stuck down. Try doing a drawing using only short straight lines in one direction. Not many lines are needed for it to 'read' as a face, for example. Scribbles and doodles are not too frightening to attempt while one is talking on the telephone or watching television. A 'feel' drawing happens when you close your eyes and feel the contours of your face with one hand, drawing what you feel with the other. This can be either on the surface of the face only or right round the head which produces a drawing with many overlapping lines and gives a sense of the form of the head.

It is a big mistake to try to translate your drawing into stitchery which closely resembles the drawing marks. When using fabrics and threads let the embroidery take over and add something else, not be a literal translation.

110 A carbon drawing by Sarah Harding made by going over a pencil sketch on paper with a sheet of carbon and more paper underneath. This is an alternative method to tracing and can be done directly onto coloured or thick paper

111 Pencil drawing by Catherine Dowden of an African woman with plaited hair

112 Blackwork embroidery by Catherine Dowden on white scrim using back stitch, darning and double running

113 *A Crowd of People Stood and Stared*
by Robin Richards.   A detail of a
drawing using areas of red and yellow
coloured pencil with overdrawing in
black ink

115 *Face* by Lynne Harris. A
10 cm × 12.7 cm (4 in. × 5 in.) panel
worked throughout in 2 strands of
cotton in greens and creams in chain,
back, stem and herringbone stitches
and knots, from a life drawing

114 A 'feely' drawing by Sally Ann
Boyd of her own face

116 (a) Drawing of part of a face
reduced to three tones
(b) A linear version of the drawing

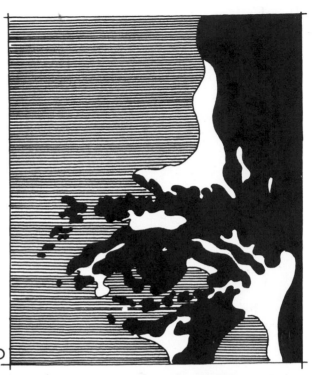

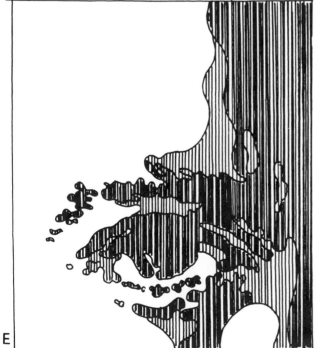

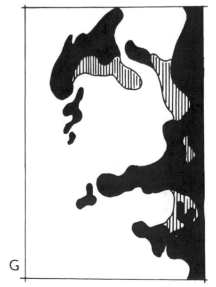

(c) Part of the face blocked out to make another design

(d) A tonal variation

(e) A version using straight lines only which leads to the embroidery

(f and g) Alternative designs

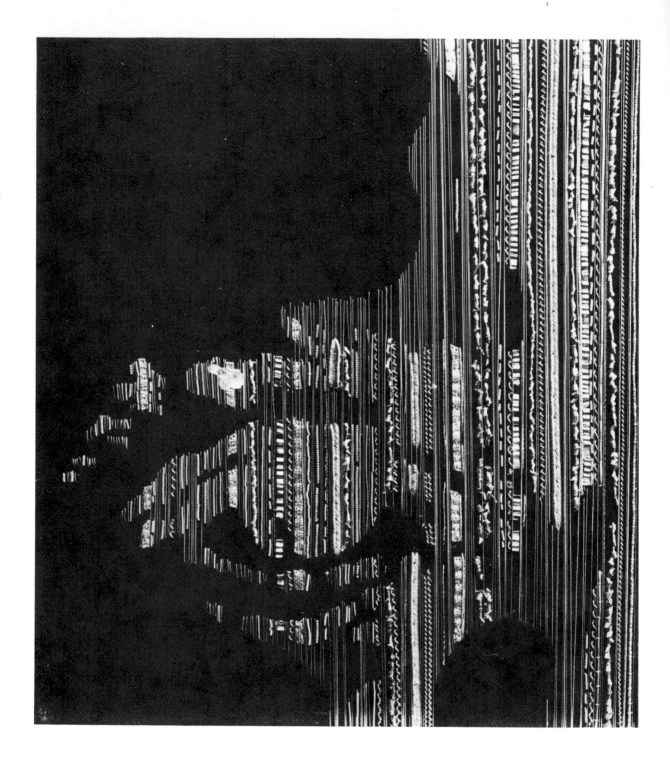

117 *Golden Eye* by Valerie Harding.
A panel worked in gold and silver on
olive green Viyella using metal threads
and purls, plate, Russia braid and
strips of leather

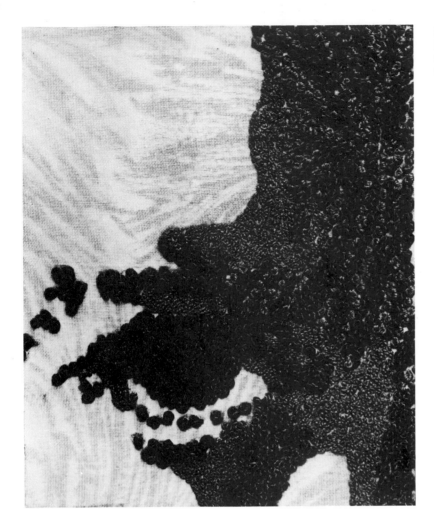

118 Another version by Valerie Harding of the same design worked entirely in french knots of different sizes on a printed fabric

Using shadows

If the shadow areas only of a face or figure are drawn on tracing paper or traced from a high contrast photograph this drawing can be used in a number of ways. The outlines of the shadows can form a basis for a quilting design, or could be carried out in linear stitchery or machine embroidery. The shadows can be filled in with black ink or felt pen on your tracing and the tracing laid over textures, patterns, a landscape or anything else to add another dimension to your original shapes. These black shapes can be cut out of card or paper and stuck to another coloured or textured paper, or onto another picture cut from a magazine, or one of your own photographs. They can be used as templates and sprayed or dabbed over with paint or dye and then the shapes peeled off to leave uncoloured areas on a coloured background. The linear version could be embroidered onto this.

91

119 Figure drawn on tracing paper with the shadows filled in with felt pen. The drawing was placed over a photograph of charred wood and the texture roughly sketched in

120 One of a set of four panels by Heather Barnard in which the face comes progressively nearer and therefore larger. Machine cording and some tufting in black, grey and lilac/grey on calico
The Oxfordshire County Museum

121 *Charlie Chaplin* by Stella Leese Canvas work using black and white wools, cotton perlé and raffia. The stitches used are rice, Florentine, tent, Smyrna, Rhodes, Norwich, diagonal satin, loops and tufting. Some of the stitching completely covers the canvas and some does not

Parts of the design can be isolated by covering up areas with pieces of paper and sometimes two or three designs can evolve from the first tracing. If you have access to a photographic dark room the tracing can be pressed firmly against sensitised paper under a sheet of glass on the baseboard of an enlarger while a negative is projected through the enlarger. The print is exposed and developed in the usual manner but only the empty areas of the tracing will show what was on the negative as the blacked-in areas have not allowed the light to reach the photographic paper.

92

A

122 Three versions of the same design showing how the emphasis changes with the change of tone. This exercise is useful for monochrome embroidery

Silhouettes

We are more aware of shape than of colour and detail is not always important, so silhouettes have great impact. They are immediately recognisable as people – even individuals can be recognised by their silhouette. This fact can be made use of when designing for embroidery as a complicated shape can be left as a plain dark shape and the background built up to add interest, colour and texture. These plain shapes can be applied pieces, holes or even filled in with simple stitchery worked either as pattern or texture and without details of the features or limbs. When a design has to be seen from a distance the strong plain shape of a silhouette will stand out from a cluttered environment.

94

B

C

A

B

123 Patterns drawn around templates which could be carried out in pulled or drawn thread, pattern darning, appliqué or surface stitchery. If a tracing of (a) is laid over (b) slightly out of register further treatments are suggested

Colour plate facing
A Rod Mask by Jean Mould.
In gold threads and leathers, with coloured wools and felts. The embroidery was worked flat on a frame with padding and string under the couching, and stuffing under the gold kid. Gold purl outlines some of the shapes. When the embroidery was finished it was removed from the frame and sewn to a moulded buckram foundation. See also figure 68 and caption

Stencils and templates

Figure shapes can be cut from card and used as templates, placing them on a sheet of paper and drawing lines or texture around them. Move the templates and draw over the texture so that it builds up in parts of the background. The same technique can be used with the negative shapes in the card that the templates were cut from, if this was done carefully with a knife. In this case the figure will be filled in with texture and the background left plain. Templates can be placed on a fabric that has been printed or painted, or on a commercial fabric print. The outline can be quilted, stitched as an outline or the shape filled in with stitchery or appliqué. Another way to use templates is to tack them to the fabric, work landscapes, scenes or patterns around them and finally remove the templates to leave a blank space. A template can be laid on a fabric, the outline tacked, and the template removed. The whole design is then filled in with lines or texture. At the edge of the figure shape the line or texture should change, either a change of colour or stitch, a change in the thickness of the line or size of the stitch, or a gap left to indicate the shape.

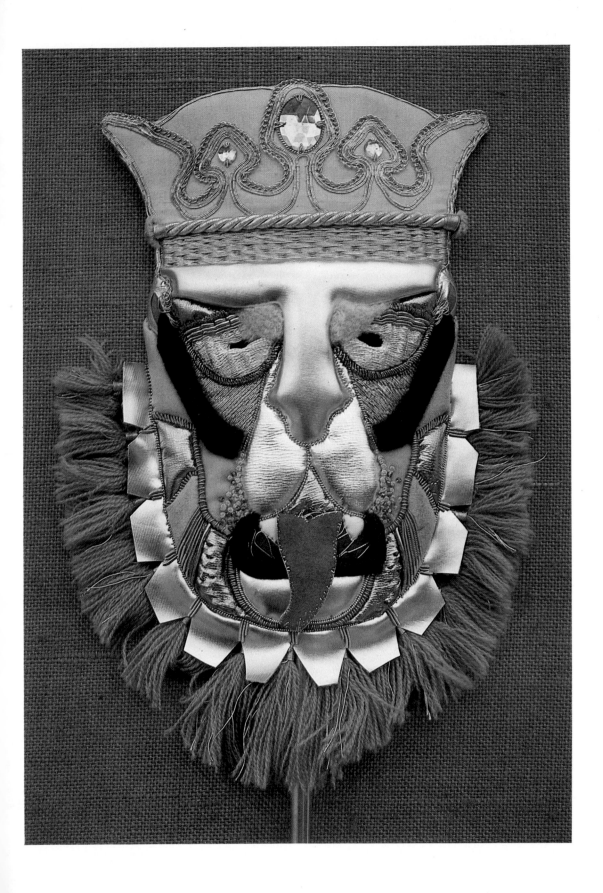

124 A silhouette with background texture which could also be lettering or patterns

Colour plate facing
Two Figures in a Garden by Julia Sorrell.
Fabric painting and patterned stitchery
The Berkshire Schools Museum
Service. See also figure 221 and caption

125 Short diagonal lines define the outline of a silhouette or template. The template was moved and more lines were drawn to give ghostly images. Longer lines were added to break up the shape and add tone. This was based on a photographic experiment by O R Croy

126 A typewriter design by Paul Harding based on a photograph of himself when a small boy

Typewriter designs

If a design is drawn onto a piece of paper no wider than the platten of a typewriter, the shape can be filled in with typed letters. The different letters make different tonal areas and they can overlap or gaps can be left. A similar effect is given by a computer print-out of a photograph, which fills in the tones with symbols and letters which are remarkably like black-work patterns.

127 A bas-relief photograph of
Paul Harding

128 A tracing of the dark areas only
of the photograph. If this tracing is
placed over the typewriter design it
adds definition

Bas-reliefs
This term is applied to shallow carvings, but also to a photographic
process when a negative and a positive version of the same subject are
printed together slightly out of register. The same effect can be
achieved by making two tracings of the same drawing in which the
tones are reversed, placing them together slightly out of register and
re-tracing either the totally clear areas or the totally black ones.

99

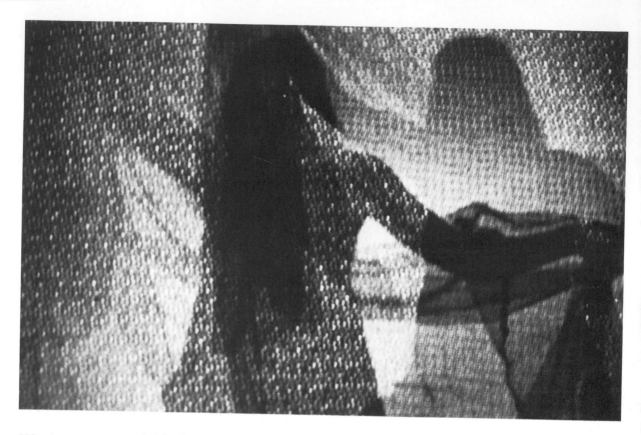

129 A transparency sandwich of a
girl and her shadow together with one
of texture

Projecting transparencies

An enlarger, a projector or an overhead projector can enlarge or
reduce designs very much more easily and accurately than any other
method. A transparency or slide, a negative or a small tracing can be
projected onto a piece of paper stuck to a wall and the enlargement
drawn from it. Two slides, or a slide and a drawing can be projected
together as a sandwich. Slides can also be projected onto shaped
objects so that one can see the effect of the lines or patterns as they are
altered by the bumps and hollows of the object. Slides can also be
projected onto a three-dimensional mock-up of card (such as a cube)
and the lines of the design drawn right onto the card.

130 A transparency of a pattern was projected onto a wig stand the curves of which distort the pattern

Patterns

A pattern is a decorative design. Repetition, either organised and regular, or informal and accidental, is a constant factor. Almost any shape or line, if repeated often enough, will form a pattern and groupings of the repeated shape or line can exist. The shapes can vary slightly within the pattern but they must be similar. The size and colour can also vary.

Rhythm gives movement to an arrangement and consists of real or imaginary lines which flow from one part of the design to another, although the shapes might not touch each other.

131 A Greek head by Jan Messent. Repeating lines and shapes forming pattern within the drawing

132 Tatoo pattern on the face of a Maori chief. This could be cut up and the parts re-arranged to make another design

133 A painted wooden mask from the Congo showing the repetition of simple lines to fill areas

102

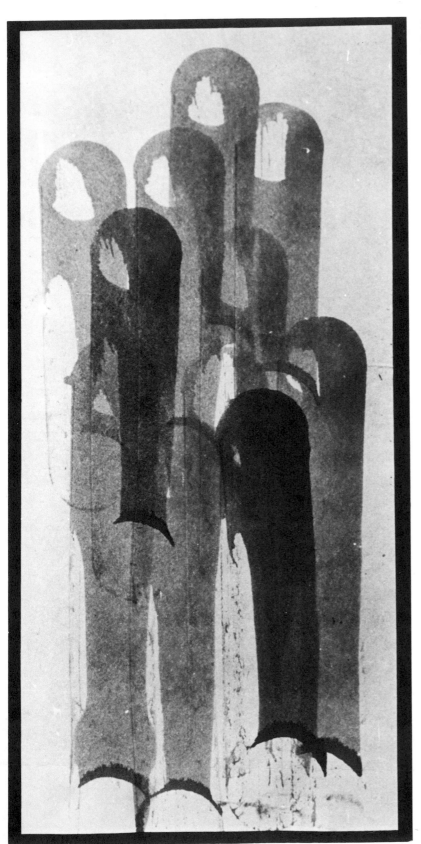

134 A group of people. A curtain ring was dipped in paint and dragged down the sheet of paper

135   An example of symmetrical pattern in this motif from a Peruvian textile *circa* AD 500

136   Two sizes of the same drawing of a Mexican carving in this design

137   (a and b) Five sizes of the drawing. This can be achieved in a projector, an enlarger or a Grant machine

A design is symmetrical when both halves correspond and the effect is rather stiff and formal. Asymmetry is more lively and one large shape can be balanced by several small ones. A change of scale within the same pattern is interesting and different sizes of the same unit can be used.

104

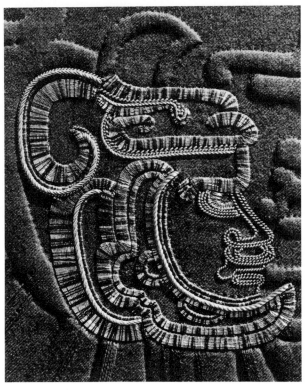

138 *Inner Man* by Valerie Harding.
Quilting and goldwork with a
patchwork border

139 Detail showing coloured
stitching over the couched gold thread
to cut the shine. The raised areas are
made by cutting the shapes in card,
gluing felt to the surface, placing it
between the fabric and the backing and
stitching the fabrics together around
the edges of the card.

Pattern can be used as a foundation of shapes which break up a
large area and link together the units that are placed within them. For
example a curtain could be divided into squares with a different face
or figure in each one.

140 (a, b and c) My daughter stood on a piece of paper and I drew around her feet. The design was reduced to a manageable size and different versions were tried of which these three seemed to have the most possibilities

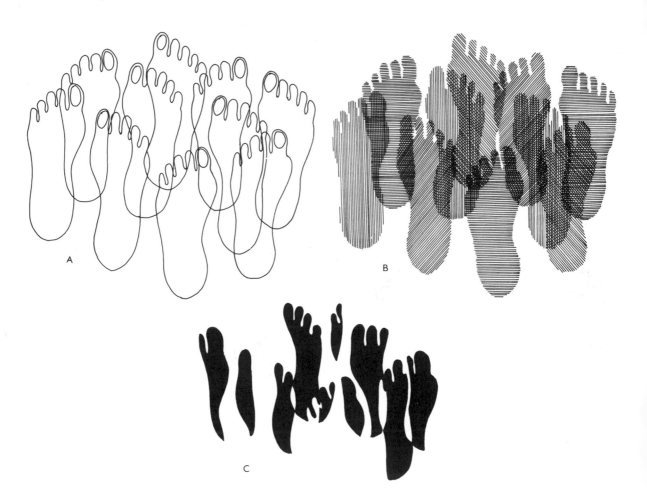

Pattern using repeating motifs

These motifs may be separate, may join, may overlap or interlock. One unit can be repeated to form an all-over design as in a crowd of people, when the sizes and shapes vary slightly but the total effect is of the similar units.

Motifs can be placed next to each other to form a line or border. Straight lines of motifs can repeat in either vertical or horizontal rows, on the diagonal, or in a grid in which the rows cross each other. These lines can also turn corners, zigzag, curve or wave and can radiate from the centre of a shape. To make a pattern turn a corner, or zigzag, hold a rectangular mirror on its edge touching the design. Place it diagonally across the border and move it about until a satisfactory arrangement is found.

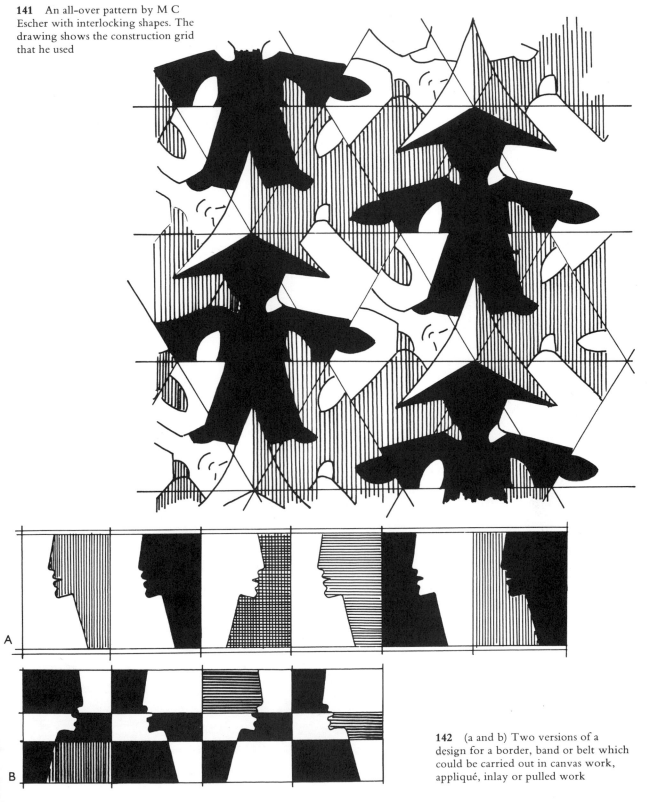

141 An all-over pattern by M C Escher with interlocking shapes. The drawing shows the construction grid that he used

A

B

142 (a and b) Two versions of a design for a border, band or belt which could be carried out in canvas work, appliqué, inlay or pulled work

107

143 An example of a vertical border pattern designed by Heide Jenkins to go up a sleeve. It is ideal for counted thread embroidery

144 Drawing by Susan Messent from an African pot in the Commonwealth Institute

145 (a and b) Border of children's figures showing how it can turn a corner

A

B

108

A face, figure, or part of a figure, can be used as the basic unit and make borders which are particularly suitable for necklines, yokes, skirts or sleeves of dresses, belts, gussets for bags or cushions, lamp-shades, down the side or along the bottom of curtains, or surrounding a central motif on a cushion or bed-spread. Rows of borders, each composed of different motifs, can be placed together to make either a wider border or an all-over pattern. These motifs could be different elements isolated from the same complex design, or they could be slightly different versions of the same unit such as a face.

146 (a and b) Drawing by Jean Littlejohn of a Chimu head with the quilted border based on it which was designed for the square neckline of a dress

109

147 (a) Drawing of a carving on an African drum in the Pitt Rivers Museum, Oxford

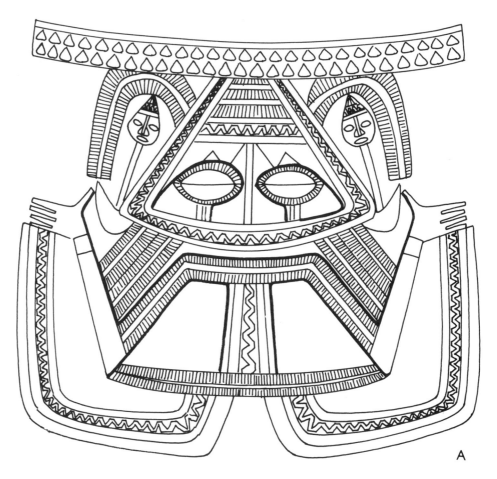

A

Repeated motifs can be placed in a more haphazard manner which can flow from one side of the design to another, as in a game of football when the players spacing and grouping varies within the field.

One way of building up a repeating pattern is by the cut paper method. The pieces can be stuck and the pattern traced. The tracing is then used to transfer the design onto fabric. The shapes can be cut through several thicknesses of paper at the same time to ensure uniformity or each one cut out separately to ensure a variation. The quickest method of repeating a motif is to block print it either from a lino or potato cut, or from a block made from small card shapes stuck to a larger piece of card. A handle is made from a folded piece of sticky tape stuck to the back. Printing allows for different groupings and colourings but ensures that the shape is constant. A slower method is to trace and re-trace the whole or parts of the motif, but more detail and some texture can be included.

110

(b, c and d) Simplified versions for
curved and straight borders. The
straight borders could be used together

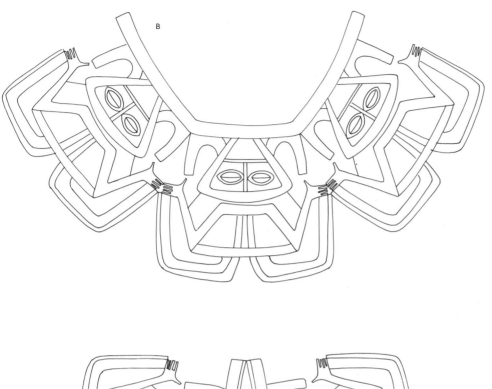

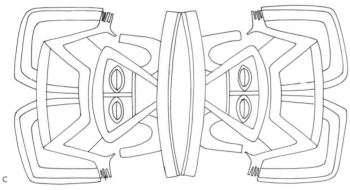

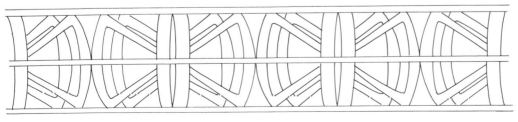

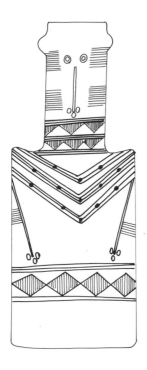

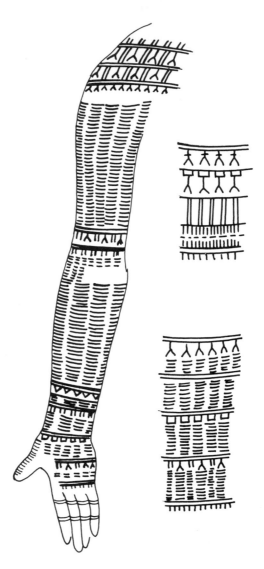

148 An incised clay figuring from Cyprus made in 1700 BC. It is a female fertility figure and was the symbol of life and rebirth. It is a suitable motif for a border

149 Arm and leg tatoo patterns of the eastern Eskimos, who often used the Y symbol

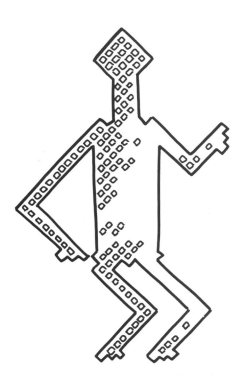

150 Diamonds filling a Congolese
figure on a woven mat

151 A chequerboard pattern projected
onto a nude figure

Designs with patterned fillings

Another way of using pattern is to fill the various areas in a design
with pattern, either in the form of stitches, or with pieces of fabric,
or such things as loops, tassels or beads. Techniques such as blackwork,
pulled thread, canvas work, patchwork, and surface stitchery can be
included in this section. Multiple lines, either straight or curved,
also make pattern and can be interpreted using line stitches, tucks or
pleats, or wrapped string. When designing for patterned areas make
use of newspaper print, rubbings and photographs of patterns such as
tiles, walls or fields of wheat, to give suggestions for the stitchery in
different areas.

152 The Man, symbol of St Matthew from the Northumbrian *Book of Dorrow*. His arms and body are covered with check patterns in red, green and yellow. *Circa* AD 680

153 *Ophelia* by Muriel Best. Patterns in stitchery and repeating lines in soft, gentle colours

114

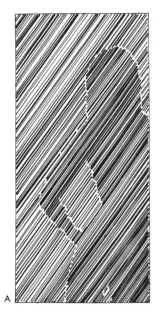

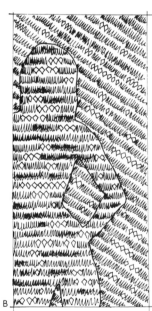

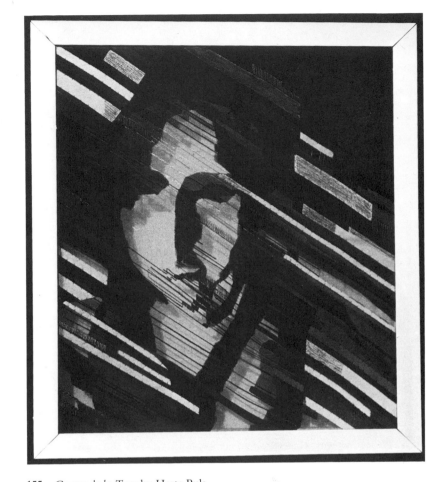

155 *George de la Tour* by Herta Puls.
The design is based on a fifteenth
century painting and the treatment is
suggested by the way a picture is built
up on a television screen. Strips of
cream and brown leather and suede
are applied to black and white organdie
with chain and straight stitches in grey
and black

154 (a and b) Two versions of the
same design which suggest different
treatments. In a the density changes at
the outline, and in b the direction alters

115

156 Detail of head by Jan Messent
shown in colour plate facing page 72

157 Drawing of a Kuba carved
wooden cosmetic box

158 Face by Lynne Harris in greys
and black on white scrim. Mainly
eyelets with satin and straight stitches
and a drawn ground

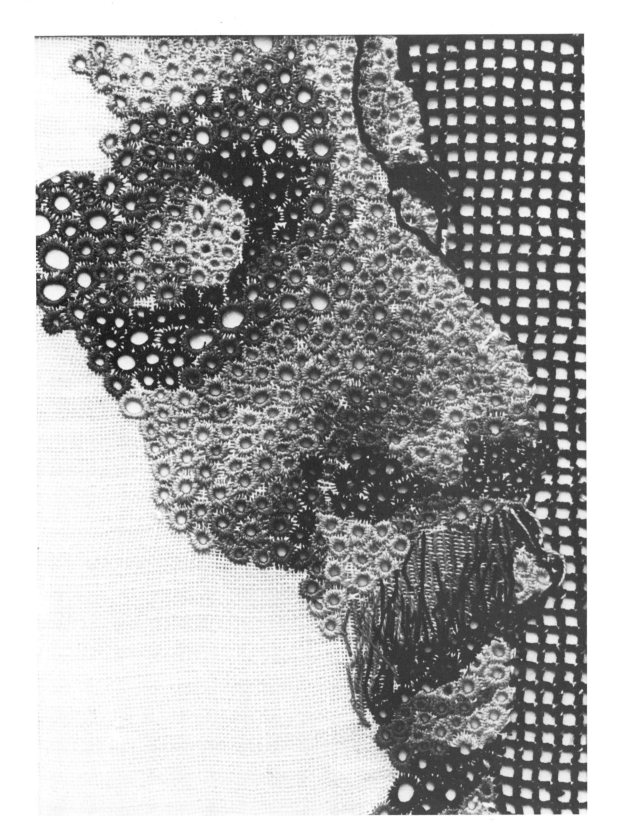

159 Blackwork face by Eileen Martin using different thicknesses of thread and interesting patterns to give tonal variation. Photograph by Frank Martin

160 Head by Henrietta Curtis in canvas work with loops, sequins and beads and flat stitches

119

Parts of
the body

Certain parts of the body can be used as a basis for a design as even a small detail, if treated with thought and feeling, can be suitable subject matter. The separate facial features, hands, skull, or a medical diagram of a human cell, can be expanded to become a design for a panel, a box lid or a border. Skulls in particular have interested many different peoples who have treated them in various ways. In France, for example, at about 300 BC skulls were built into stone doorposts of the temples as a protection against supernatural danger. Skulls have been painted, covered with gold or precious stones or with mosaic, or, in central America, are modelled in sugar for festivals.

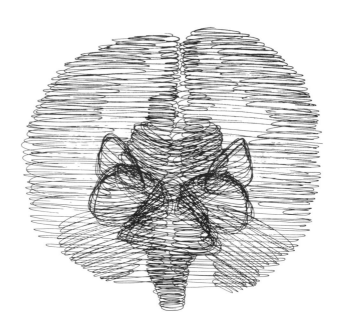

161 Drawing of a computer photograph of a brain

120

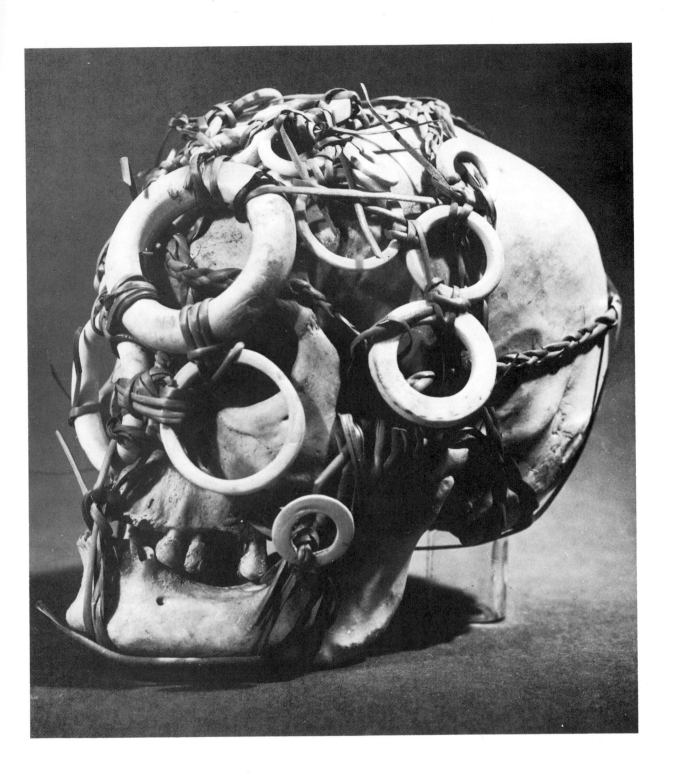

162 An African skull with bone
rings laced to it with cane
The Pitt Rivers Museum, Oxford

163 A lip print made by pressing lips painted with a dark lipstick onto a piece of paper

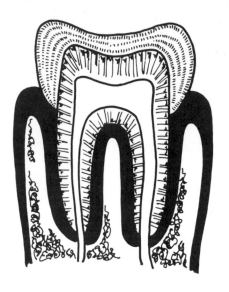

164 A cross section of a tooth which could easily be developed into a border pattern

Racial characteristics

The variations between races of people of their facial and bodily characteristics should be studied so that when these peoples are depicted in an embroidery they are convincing. Of course some personal characteristics cut across what is imagined to be the racial ones, but in an embroidery the main racial differences will probably take precedence over the personal ones.

Mouths

The mouth and lips are supposed to indicate qualities such as firmness, meanness, viciousness, a love of pleasure or precision and so on. Large lips are supposed to indicate indolence or sensuality. Negroid races tend to have thicker lips than Europeans, but one cannot imagine that all negroes are indolent, so in this case the racial characteristic is predominant.

The mouth breathing fire was often mentioned in ancient literature and this suggests subject matter for a design. Mouths and lips kiss, eat, form words, smile or pout, and can be painted or tatooed. In Maori art great emphasis is placed on the tongue which can be very long indeed and decorated with patterns.

122

165 A collection of eyes in many different styles suitable for different embroidery methods

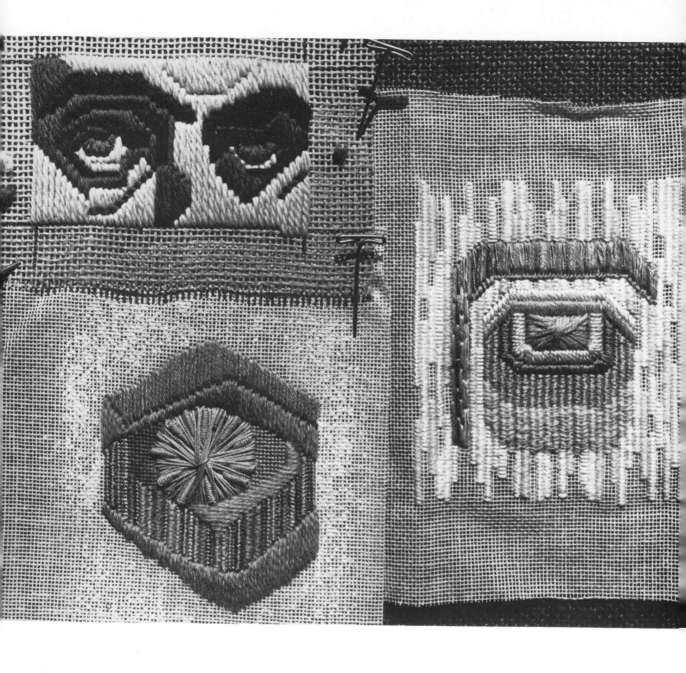

166 Canvas work eyes. (The one at the top left is by Anne Dyer and the other two by Valerie Harding)

167 A design for an eye based on a photograph of an eye printed together with a line pattern

Eyes

Eyes are often the most powerful indication of character and are generally the focal point of the face. Make-up around the eyes serves to make them seem larger and even more interesting and eye decoration as used in different civilizations or in the theatre can suggest many ways to emphasize the eyes when embroidering a face. Eyes can also be subject matter in their own right.

Pale eyes usually go with light coloured hair and vice versa, and people from hot climates have darker eyes than people from colder areas. The different colours are all produced by varying quantities of only one pigment, which is brown. At different times eyebrows have been shaved, plucked or darkened, and this gives a characteristic look to the face which must be taken into account. To the ancient Egyptians the eye symbolised the power of the sun, and eyes which appear on unusual parts of the body in the paintings or carvings of many peoples bestow power on that part. In some cultures the whole of life is thought to be lived under the watchful eye of the spirits of dead ancestors. Extra eyes were once believed to bestow extra spiritual powers, and to have three eyes was divine.

In a design the eye is often enlarged to give it importance. If the eyes are embroidered in an interesting manner, and not just indicated with a knot or a bead, then the rest of the features can play a secondary role. Bags under the eye, folds of skin around it, the distance between the eyes or between the eye and brow, and the angle the eye is set at, all help to give it individuality and only a slight variation of one of these aspects will make a surprising difference.

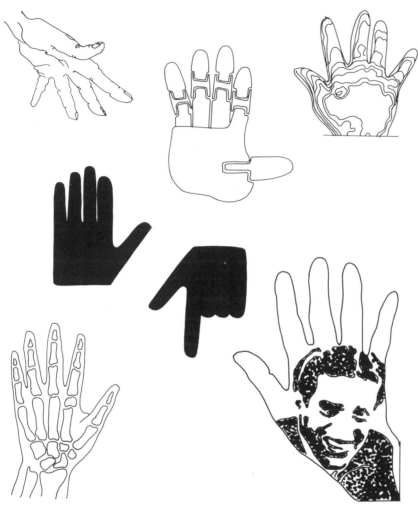

168 Hands, including a drawing, a mechanical hand, a heat map, hands from signs, the bone structure and a design symbolising discrimination

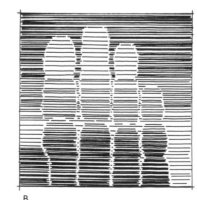

169 A three-dimensional model of St Lachtin's arm in bronze, silver, gold, copper and glass on a wood core

A

B

170 (a) Stylised drawing of my own hand
(b) A version suitable for embroidery

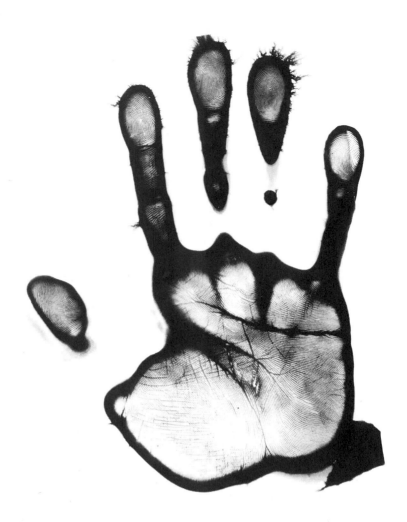

171 A print made by Paul Harding by pressing a hand soaked in fixer onto sensitised paper before developing it

Hands and feet

We use our hands so much that we forget to look at them closely, but they are always with us and can be drawn easily. Hands and feet can make printing marks, be drawn around, be pressed into plasticine to make a mould, or be held in a number of different positions against the light to make a silhouette. It is obviously difficult to photograph one's own hands but other people are not so embarrassed at having their hands photographed as they are their faces or bodies. Keep an eye out for pointing hands on signs, for hands doing different jobs such as spinning or playing the piano, or for relaxed hands at rest on the arms of a chair.

Because legs and feet are down below us they are also often forgotten, but rows of legs in a bus queue with shopping bags and baskets, or footprints around a swimming pool or in sand, could be explored as subject matter. On Adam's Peak in Ceylon is the legendary footprint in stone of the Buddha. (It does not seem to worry anyone that the print is about 2 metres–7 feet long.) This is the symbol of the imprint left on the island by Buddhism.

172 Drawing of a foot

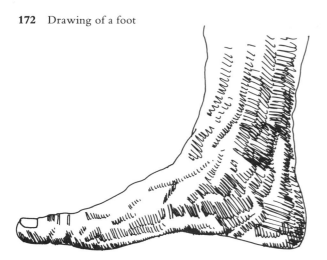

173 Ghostly images of dancing feet and swirling skirts

174 Stylised drawing of the footprint of the Buddha from a book cover

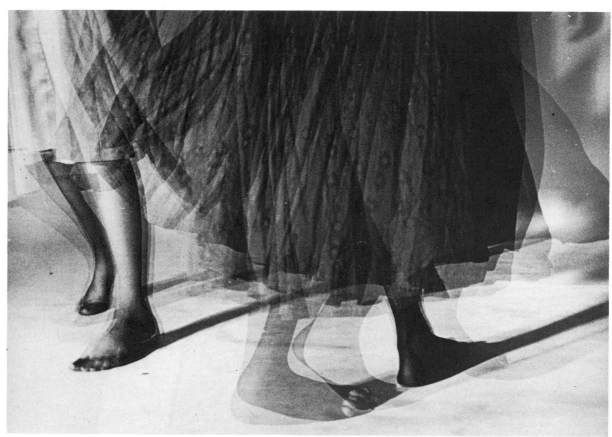

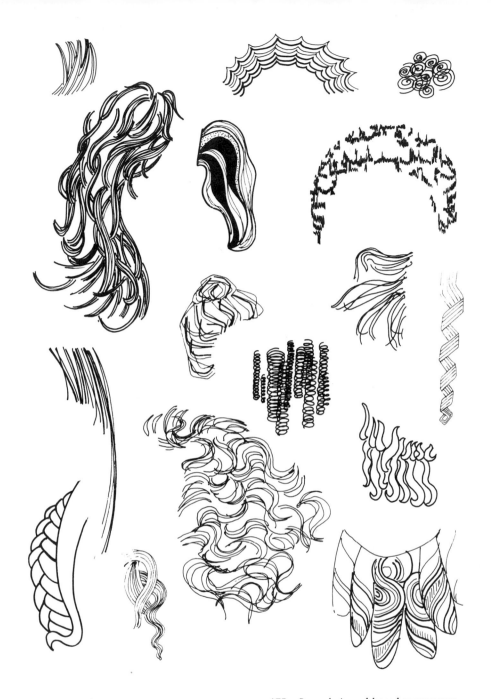

Hair

Hair can be straight and smooth as in China, wavy and curly as in Europe, woolly or frizzy as in Africa, depending on whether the individual hairs are a flat oval or round. Hair comes in many colours but is very seldom a flat colour all over. Red hair in particular seems to have yellow, blue, red or green in it at times. People have and do bleach and dye their hair to change the colour to one that they prefer and sometimes this is dictated by custom. During the Crusades auburn was the colour of a witch's hair, and in ancient Greece prostitutes' hair was bright yellow.

175 Some hair and beard treatments

129

176 Panel by Jane Clark featuring hair with scrim and chiffon on a painted calico background. The chiffon has been pulled up through slits in the calico. Needleweaving, machine looping and straight stitches add texture

Hair styles are most interesting to study and if you are depicting people from other times or parts of the world they should be accurate. Many styles can be used as inspiration for ways to embroider hair and ringlets, buns or plaits on an African are examples. Wigs have been used to make the hair more voluminous or to alter the colour and can be very intricately styled.

177 Detail of a doll by Joan Hake showing the embroidered features and the hair which is made of two layers of macramé braids lying in different directions

131

178 A bronze head of Sargon the Great who lived about 2250 BC and founded the Akkadian empire in Mesopotamia. This drawing shows intricate hair treatment which was bound with a band, and a curled beard

179 An embroidery by Jean Littlejohn from the same source. Quilted white calico with buttonhole loops, twisted cords, fringing and interlacing

Beards have been widely regarded through the ages as a sign of strength and virility and wisdom. They have been plaited, curled, shaped, glued into elaborate designs or even gilded.

The face

There has been a constant fascination with the human face since time out of mind. Often we see what we want to see rather than what is there and it is amazing how often we imagine we see a face in clouds, leaves and branches, the moon or rocks. This image seems to take precedence over all others when there is a shortage of visual information. This fascination is reflected in embroidery and the face is often used as the subject of a panel, book cover, box lid or on dress.

Two, three or more faces can be used together in a design that can be more interesting than when there is only a single one. Different sizes of faces, different views and angles, or parts of faces with whole faces are all aspects worth consideration at the planning stage.

180 *Man Emerging* The patchwork background represents the strata, the next layer of padded shapes represents the planets, and finally Man. Commercial dolls' faces are covered with stretch fabric and quilted

181 A design using masks with the background to be built up in layers. The masks will be in relief. Some of the dark areas will be fabric and some in solid stitchery

182 *Egyptian Heads* by Patricia
Lyford.   Nets on slub linen with
machine embroidery and couching.
The Berkshire Schools Museum
Service

183 *Heads* by Jocelyn Barnes.   This
panel illustrates how successful the
simplest shapes are for embroidery. It
is worked in gold threads and cords,
purls and braids with yellow, turquoise
and royal blue threads on a dark green
background.
The Oxford County Museum

135

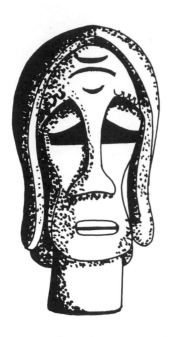

Looking at a face through a Venetian blind, through textured glass or a bottle, or through a grill alters and fragments the face in an interesting manner. Patterns in carved faces, tatoo marks and the layers of the facial muscles all suggest techniques or stitchery to interpret the design.

The variations in the human face are limitless and are affected by the technique used to portray it. If designing a face using strips of paper or string, the results will obviously be very different from a face that is drawn from life, and the face will and should hold this style through the subsequent embroidery.

Features can be a problem to embroider, but less so if considered in relation to the rest of the design. Sometimes one or more of the features can be left out altogether if it is thought that the face is complete without it. The eyes should be worked first, then the mouth and then other details such as nose, character lines or a beard added. Faces can be left totally blank for the sake of anonymity or if the design is on a very small scale.

184 A carved wooden puppet head of a sorrowing woman

Facial expression

The size and position of the features in relation to each other and the shape of the face are the first decisions to make. Then the expression and detail can be worked. The human face is very mobile owing to more than a hundred different muscles lying just below the surface of the skin. These make possible the many different and very subtle expressions of which a face is capable. One of the most difficult things to embroider is a realistic face with the right expression as the placing of a single stitch can alter it. Such things as the angle of the brows, how wide open the eyes are and the curve of the mouth, however slight, all alter the expression.

Qualities perceived in faces are obviously influenced by the personality of the viewer and the less defined the features are the more the viewer projects into the expression of the face.

185 An eighteenth century Japanese sword guard with a very fierce, angry expression on the face

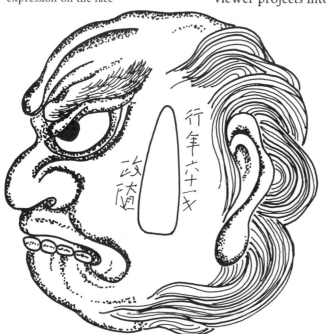

行年六十六
政隨

186 This face by Margaret Turner shows indifference and serenity. Blues and greens with some gold. Velvet ribbon, braids, applied fabrics and jewels with some stitchery

188 A long suffering look on the face of this African man who is waiting patiently

189 *Hanging Warrior* by Jan Messent. A haughty expression is perfectly captured on the face mainly because of the eyes. Padding with extra pieces applied on top which are stuffed. Reproduced by permission of Mrs N Fletcher

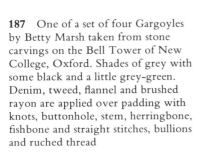

187 One of a set of four Gargoyles by Betty Marsh taken from stone carvings on the Bell Tower of New College, Oxford. Shades of grey with some black and a little grey-green. Denim, tweed, flannel and brushed rayon are applied over padding with knots, buttonhole, stem, herringbone, fishbone and straight stitches, bullions and ruched thread

190 Side view of *Hanging Warrior* showing the patchwork helmet, tufted hair and plaited beard

191 *A Young Girl* by Briony Neilson
in blackwork on white scrim using
threads of various weights

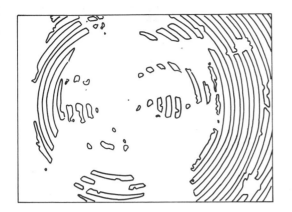

192 *A Young Girl* A drawing of a photograph by O R Croy in which a negative of a girl is printed sandwiched with one of concentric circles. The shapes would be filled in with applied leather or fabric, or stitchery, or it could be quilted

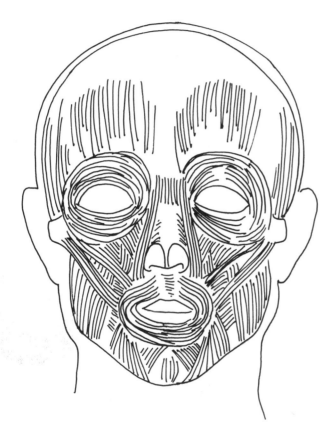

193 The muscle patterns on the face. This suggests direction of stitchery or couched gold threads

Age

Youth or old age can be indicated by the facial proportions, the smoothness of the skin, the colouring and also by size. There is a certain amount of fatty tissue under the skin which gradually disappears towards middle age and causes wrinkling. These wrinkles tend to occur at right angles to the muscles of the face. Pouches and bags can appear to break up the smooth areas of the forehead and cheeks, and sometimes the mouth sinks in and this causes the nose to overhang. Eyes seem smaller because of the folds of skin around them. Young faces are more difficult to draw and to embroider and older ones are usually more interesting with their lines of character.

195 *An Old Man* by Briony Neilson
in machine embroidery and stuffed
quilting

194 *Old Woman* by Audrey Ormrod
in quilting through layers of fabric and
wadding on a *papier mâché* base

196 A Tsimshian carved wooden
mask. A stylised representation of a
very old man with bags and lined skin

197 *A Sailor* This type of drawing suggests the use of burden stitch, either in gold or coloured threads, or blackwork

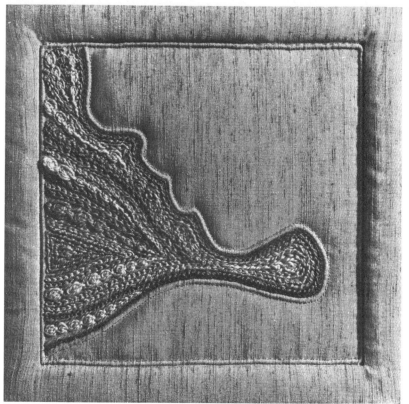

198 An ancient Egyptian profile which is doll-like

199 *Young Girl* by Molly Taylor. Padding, with string under the fabric to define the edge. The background is filled in with stem, chain and rosette chain in purples and mauves on mauve furnishing fabric

200 A pendant by Julia Roberts with cotton fabrics applied to velvet, machine stitching and gold beads

201 *Centurion* by Jenny Blackburn. A batik cotton with padding and stitchery

202 Book-box. This was made to keep the reference material for this book in. When the cord at the front of the box is untied the sides fall away to allow easy access to the contents

The profile

A profile is more interesting in outline than the full face and can be easier to draw. There is less detail and the problem of balancing the two halves does not arise. A profile of someone you know can be drawn on tracing paper taped to a window or sheet of glass with the person standing on the other side of the glass. The light should be behind the person to show up the outline clearly. Victorian silhouettes were often of profiles, usually without any detail, but occasionally a small amount was added, such as part of an eye or ear, or some locks of hair.

203 (a and b) Two drawings of a
solarised photograph

146

The three-quarter face

Looking at faces from angles other than from the front or the side is more unusual and sometimes more interesting. One can walk around a statue or a person to see which angle is the most effective and then take a photograph for reference. Drawing someone asleep in a chair or while they are occupied with something means that they do not get bored posing for you. The shape and size of the eyes is different from an angle and also the cheeks. One can look from above or below a face or partly from one side. A composition in which there are many faces with their heads turned so that you see them from different angles will be more vital than one in which all the faces are viewed from one direction only.

147

204 A possible layout for a panel. Variety could be introduced with a change of tone and colour and the type of threads used

205 This photograph by Anne Dyer shows how much interest there can be in a simple treatment of a face. The negative spaces are given full value and also the contrast between single and multiple lines. Plastic cord stitched to furnishing fabric

148

206 *Pan* by Beryl Court. Cream
stockinette applied to brown hessian
with some covered card shapes on top
of the nose and cheeks. Ginger, cream,
rust and fawn wools are looped and
made into braids, picots and
buttonhole loops

149

207 *Head of Christ* by Jessy Curette.
Pale grey Thai silk with silver kid
thorns. The face is worked in vertical
rows of split stitch with coloured
stitching to indicate modelling. The
hair is couched threads pulled from a
silk fabric

The full face
Most people draw or design a face while looking at it directly from
the front and think of it as perfectly symmetrical. However it is not
as is found when two identical but reversed photographs of a face are
cut down the middle and the two right halves married together and
then the two left halves. The result will look rather like two similar
people neither of which matches the original. Slight variation in the
size and placing of the features make the original face look less
wooden.

150

208 A cutwork head by Joan Hake
in pale green linen based on a drawing
of a Yemeni woman in a head-dress.
Eyelets, buttonhole, couching, raised
chain band, Portuguese knotted stem,
knots, fly stitch and spiders' webs in
green threads

209 A box with three faces in gold on cream fabric by Valerie Harding. Various threads and purls are used with small pieces of applied mustard silk. The box is lined with the same silk

210 *The Bath Gorgon* by Penelope Cuthbert.   Painting on cream calico with padding and peach chiffon pulled through slits in the calico. Couched cream weaving threads, straight stitches and needleweaving

211   An unfinished box top with a doll's face and polystyrene shapes held between two layers of fabric. Some wrapped threads and stiff plastic cords have been added. This is reminiscent of the stumpwork period when wooden or wax face moulds were used and covered with stitchery or satin

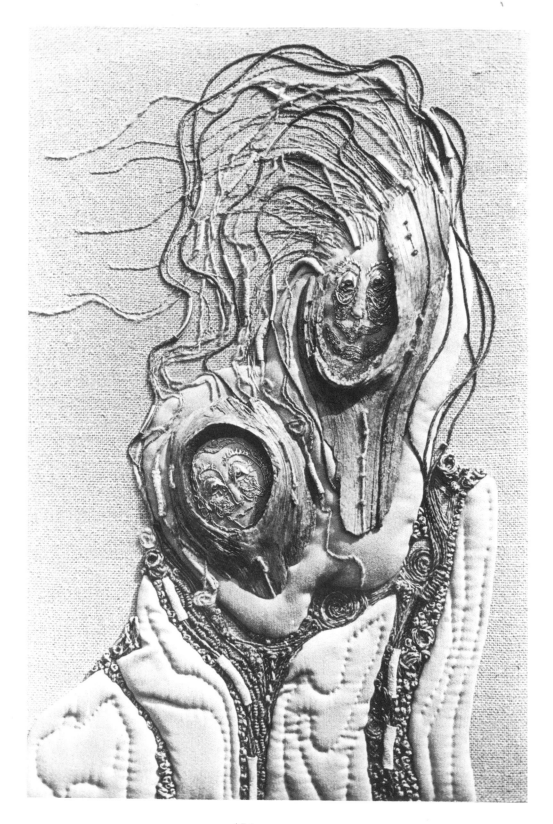

154

212 *Pollarded Tree Conversation* by Julie Athill. Blue grey fabric with pieces of wood supporting the faces which are embroidered in gold. Brown garden string and blue-grey threads are stitched and knotted on the hessian ground

213 A face in Casalguidi embroidery by Kit Pyman with highly raised stitching on a drawn-fabric ground

There is a universal desire to alter the face, sometimes in the pursuit of beauty, sometimes to differentiate one person from another or to add status. Tatooing is one method of doing this and face painting is another. Both these can suggest ways of breaking up the face into areas or pattern and can be adapted for stitchery. If the plain areas of cheek and forehead are broken up with pattern or stitches then try to make them slightly different in each half of the face. It is not necessary to include the whole face in a design and strips of paper can block out unwanted parts until a pleasing composition is reached.

If a strong light is shone on a face from different angles the face is altered considerably without any actual change of expression. When the light is shone from below it adds eeriness, if from above it adds years onto the age of the face. If the light comes from one side it blocks out irrevelant detail and makes the two sides seem different from each other. The shape of the shadows add form to the face.

155

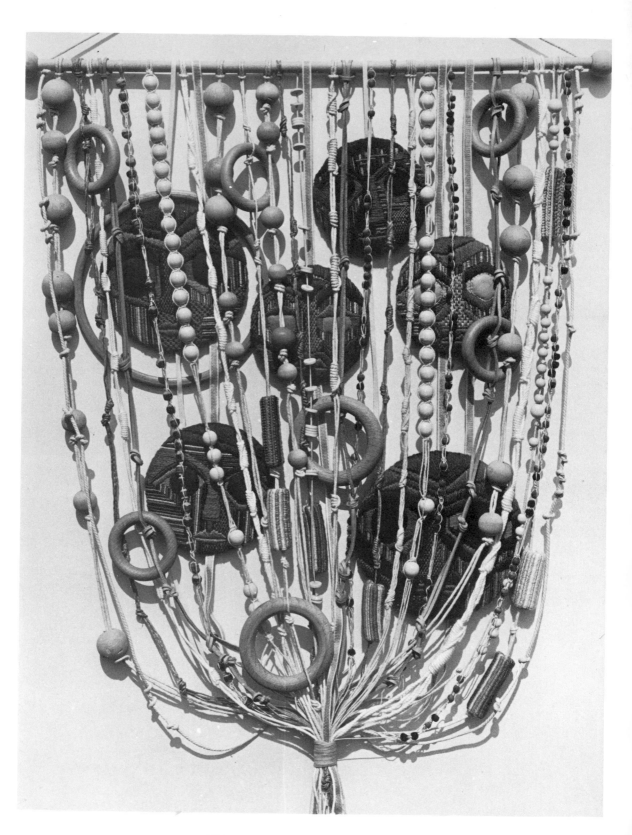

214 *Staring People* by Valerie Harding. These are faces of bored people staring through a 'bead' curtain at the rest of the world passing by. Canvas work faces and knotting. Pieces of polythene tubing have been covered with canvas work

215 Detail of *Staring People*

216 *Pink Person*   A three-dimensional piece in canvas work and felt in shades of pinks and some reds. The centre disc lifts out to show a quilted version of the same face underneath. This signifies that all this person's personality is on show and that his inner self has nothing further of interest to offer

The figure

When planning an embroidery using full-length figures, whether for Ecclesiastical purposes or otherwise, the age and sex of the figures must be born in mind as men and women often hold themselves in different positions. An older person does not stand up so straight and a pregnant woman leans back slightly to balance the extra weight she is carrying. The job that people do and the customs of the society in which they live affect their positions, and the builds of thin or fat people cause them to move and hold themselves differently. A relaxed figure slopping in a chair is another problem from one who is trying to push or pull an object with the resulting tension. This is often too much to tackle so simple designs using less realistic forms can be attempted and often this gives more scope for the embroidery.

217 *Gossiping Women* by Jill Cooper. Appliqué using fabrics of different textures with couching

218 *Old Woman Bathing Child* by
Audrey Ormrod.   Pulled work and
darning in white, creams and browns
on linen scrim

219 *Pelops and the Pelopids* by Richard Box.   Pelops is riding the chariot at the top left of the panel, also Agamemnon sacrificing his daughter, and the standing figure is Hermes. At the bottom left is Clytemnestra with Agamemnon being chopped up. At the bottom right are Orestes and Electra killing his mother and her lover and in the centre is Orestes pursued by the Furies. Appliqué with couching in many shades of red, black and gold

161

220 (a) *Warriors and Eagles* by Valerie Harding. Abstract figures and winged figures in blues and greens with some pink and purple using laid work, crochet, ruched threads, buttonhole rings and needleweaving, with fabric covered card to raise some of the threads

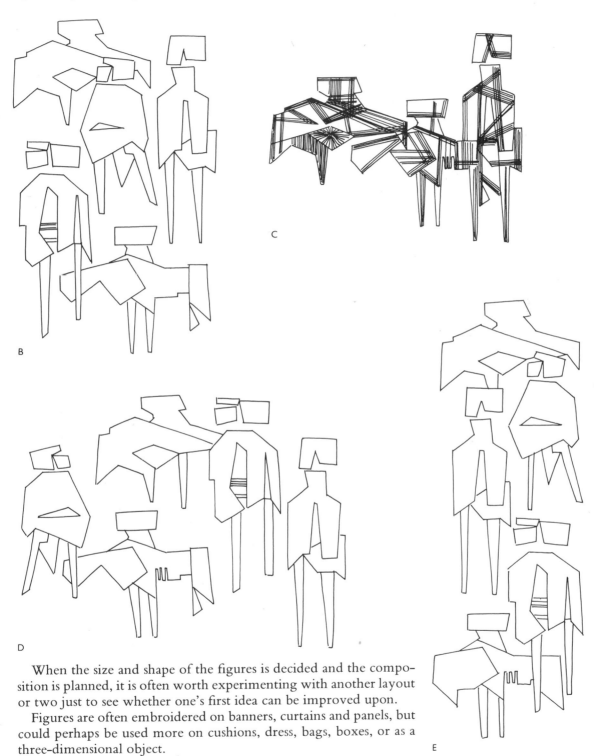

C

B

D

When the size and shape of the figures is decided and the composition is planned, it is often worth experimenting with another layout
or two just to see whether one's first idea can be improved upon.

Figures are often embroidered on banners, curtains and panels, but
could perhaps be used more on cushions, dress, bags, boxes, or as a
three-dimensional object.

E

221 *Two Figures in a Garden* by Julia
Sorrell.   Fabric dye was painted onto
fine canvas in flat areas and stitchery
was worked on top using split stitch,
couching, feather, cross and buttonhole.
Berkshire Schools Loan Service see also
colour plate facing page 97

Half figures
These are sometimes easier to fit into a composition and most of the
interest is in the top half of the body. People sit in buses and cinemas,
eat at tables, play chess or a piano, or make–up their faces in front of a
mirror. All of these suggest subjects for embroidery.

164

222 *Snake Charmer* by Jean Parry. Appliqué with some padding using nets, leathers and fabrics, beads and stitchery

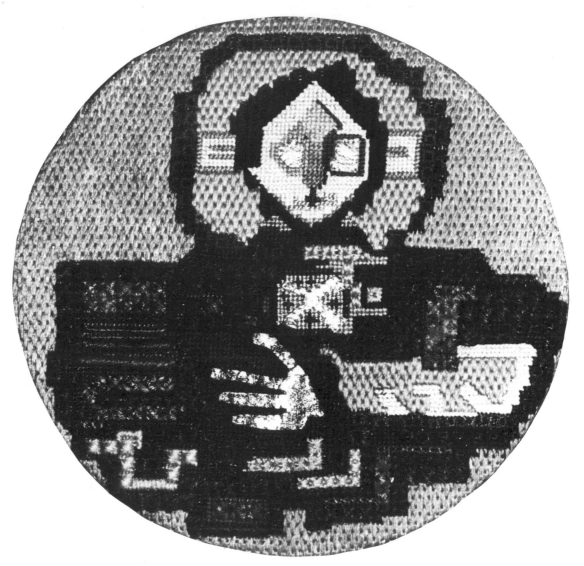

223 Detail of Canvas work figure by Catherine Dowden based on a Coptic textile

A half figure seems more intimate than a full-length one, and more detail seems necessary with a closer view point cutting out non-relevant background information. Hands are often important and the arms which link them to the shoulders and lead the eye to the face which is usually the focal point of the design.

Using different sizes of figures, such as a mother and child, adds interest. People sitting on chairs of different heights, or one figure bending over, or people in tiers, solves the problem of having more than one face at the same height.

166

224 *A Soldier* by Lynn Harris, with an interesting use of simple stitchery and voided spaces. Chain stitch and knots in wine on cream linen

225 Drawing from a photograph of my son in a denim jacket. The photograph was taken by him using the delayed action timer on his camera

226 A tracing from a newspaper photograph simplifying the tones by Jenny Bullen

227 *Reclining Nude* by Penelope Cuthbert. Brown and beige straight stitching on calico with padding in some areas

Nudes and nakedness

For the past 100 years or so the word nude has conjured up the image of a naked woman. Before this period most nudes were male. At certain times there was belief in man's divinity, and at others a curiosity about the structure of the body. Artists painted or sculpted the body in a manner which was idealistic or lifelike, sometimes both together. It has been a subject which has absorbed many artists for a long time.

The male nude has often been the symbol of a wide range of moral, religious or political meanings, whereas the female nude has usually been associated with passivity and an object of desire.

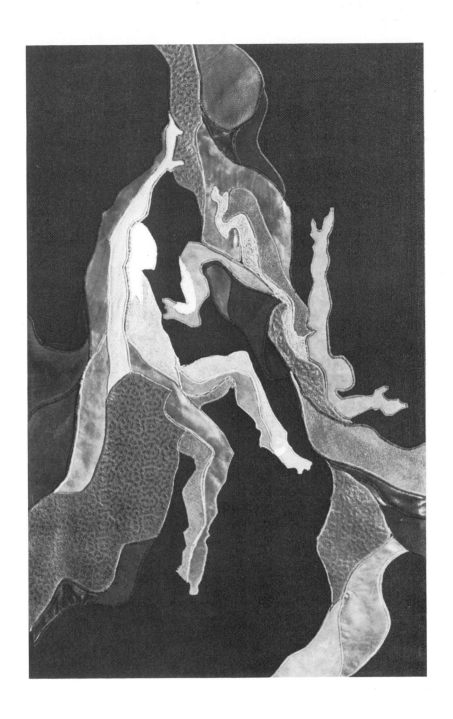

228 *Seraphim* by Richard Box.
One of a series of flying angels using
leather and suedes on a hessian
background. The shapes were applied
with machine satin stitch
The Embroiderers' Guild

In our society to see a naked body can alarm, provoke guilt or satisfy curiosity. Most people shy away from these feelings and are self-conscious about nakedness and prefer to depict people with clothes on. In other cultures where nakedness is the norm no-one is as interested in it nor do they have such mixed emotions about it.

170

The formal conventions about nudity in art vary a great deal at different times and sometimes the nude was only acceptable when it was stylised or abstracted. This attitude can result in empty formulae which provide an excuse for not really looking at the individual body. However if abstraction arises from real investigation into the whole or parts of the body this is probably more suitable to the various embroidery methods than too much realism.

230 Detail of an unfinished panel on a theme of *Men and Machinery* by Valerie Harding. The 50 mm (2 in.) figures are made of felt glued to card which are satin stitched to the background with one strand of cotton. The pipes are in couched gold threads, wrapped ice lolly sticks which have been dampened and curved and wrapped wires

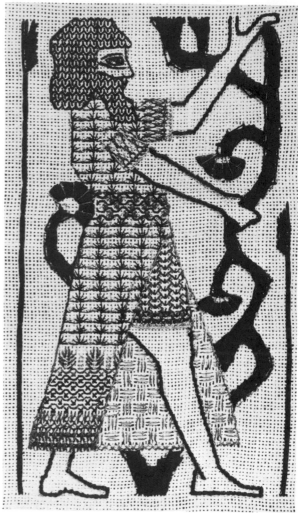

231 *Japanese Lady* by Jenny Blackburn.
On a background of batik cotton,
fabrics have been applied and some
hand and machine stitchery added

232 An Egyptian figure by Mary
Hamilton-Fairley in blackwork with
black, red and gold on cream linen

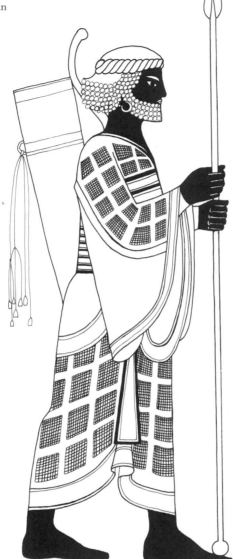

233 Drawing by Jan Messent of one of the figures in the frieze of archers painted on a tiled wall in an Assyrian palace

Clothes and costume

A study of costume is outside the scope of this book but looking at clothes of other times and places can suggest designs and the treatment of them. We are now acutely aware of history and books and museums provide plenty of reference. This knowledge of costume is fairly recent as even in the middle ages it was thought that anyone from a past time wore the Roman kilt, and anyone from far away wore a turban. This was the beginning of the custom of the Three Kings in Turkish dress. For accuracy we have to rely on sculpture and paintings of the time and illuminated manuscripts. Much costume is very decorative and on occasion very grand and lavish.

234 An embroidery by Sheila Kinross from the same source using fabric printing on gold furnishing fabric with needleweaving, spiders' webs, couching, knots and cords in rusts, grey blue, beige and mustard

235 *Flower People* by Kate Cooper.
A patchwork and appliqué hanging
using simple shapes for stylised figures.
Oxfordshire County Museum

236 A woman in grey cheesecloth
with grey satin, yellow net, couched
threads and cords by Jean Littlejohn

Clothes are made to be worn by people with bodies and limbs and this fact should be remembered while designing the figures. It is better to work out the position of the figure and then to build the clothes on and around it than to just draw a head and a robe of indeterminate length and many folds. The dressed figure must be convincing.

237 A girl made from padded card shapes covered with fabric, woven bodice, suede hair and quilted face and background by Heide Jenkins

175

238 A brass rubbing of a knight and
his lady

239 A three-dimensional Knight by Jane Lemon based on the brass rubbing using a rag doll made of calico, with cream fabric and patent leather and gold stitchery for the armour

Armour

From about 3000 BC men wore leather helmets and tunics as protection in battle and for special occasions the helmets were of copper or gold. The Greeks were the first to make considerable use of metal body armour and this was made of bronze and, later, iron. The Romans wore leather, mail, scale or lorica armour. The scales were made of overlapping metal plates fastened to a leather tunic. Lorica armour is the best known and was made of a number of metal strips which circled the body from the waist up and crossed over the shoulders. The Vikings wore coats of mail and metal helmets and so did the Normans, although of a different design.

240   Detail of the face showing the detached buttonhole mail

241   Detail of the gauntlets and the sword belt

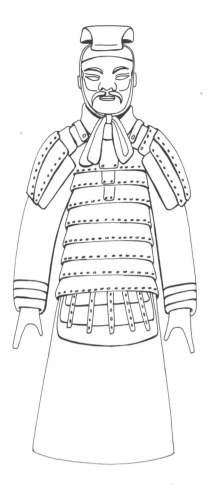

243 A design for a puppet based on a terracotta model of a Chinese warrior of 2000 BC. The body armour is of overlapping leather plates with studs, and secured with straps on the apron. The sleeves and skirt are quilted and the helmet is of folded fabric tied with a band under the chin

242 Eighteenth century Japanese armour made in the fourteenth century style
Victoria and Albert Museum, London

The complete mail suits of the mounted Crusaders sometimes weighed about 18 kg (40 lb), but the foot soldiers only had leather jackets which were re-inforced with small metal plates. As weapons became more deadly mail was replaced by plate armour with shaped pieces for the various parts of the body and this was common by the beginning of the fifteenth century. It was sometimes decorated with engraving or embossing or ornamented with silver, gold and precious stones.

179

244 Russian stacking dolls by
Beverley Crawshaw in goldwork,
beading, appliqué and surface stitchery.
Each doll is a different colour and
technique and they fit inside each
other.
The Berkshire Schools Loan Service

245 A design for a free standing doll.
The shape is based on an Irish twelfth
century bell

246 *Grotto* by Jane Livingstone. A large panel with fabric over a chicken wire foundation nailed to a wooden board. All cream with knitting, stockinette, machine tufting on calico, and weaving threads

247 A detail of one of the figures in the grotto made of pipe cleaners covered with knitted fabric

Three-dimensional figures

Dolls, puppets, chessmen or life-size soft sculptures of people all demand thought about the type of construction used to make them. Rag dolls can be any size from fairly small to larger than life and can be the basis for any figure or group of figures. The larger they are the stronger must be the fabric and stitching, and unless they are going to sit flopping in a chair, large dolls might be better if they are wired. On the other hand too small a doll is difficult to make and dress, and a convenient size would be about a metre (two or three feet) in length.

248 A hanging doll by Anne Dyer
based on a drawing of a Hopi Indian
doll, in felt, leather and fabric with
beads, stitching and feathers

Three-dimensional figures can be built up on card constructions
such as cones, cylinders or rectangles and the card base should be very
firm indeed. Each section could be covered separately and sewn
together as when making a box, or the card and fabric constructions
each finished and the fabric cover pulled over the card, then glued,
laced or sewn in place. Chicken wire is quite a good foundation for
very large heads and figures but it is not very firm. It is easy to mould
into shape and can be sewn through, so it is useful on occasion.

Puppets can be hand, rod or string puppets. Glove or hand puppets
are the simplest needing only a dress or shirt fixed to a head. The head
could be wood, *papier mâché* or a tennis ball, covered with fabric
gathered into the neck to form a frill to which the clothes are attached.
Rod puppets have slim rods attached to their hands and a thicker
main holding rod extending downwards from the head. These rods
are concealed by hanging sleeves, robes or cloaks. String puppets can
be made of wood or using a rag doll construction. They can also be
made from such scrap material as detergent bottles cut to shape and
plastic tubes for arms. Obviously these will be covered.

183

249 Detail of the face of *Winter* a rod puppet by Jean Littlejohn. Padded felt with wool and mohair beard and hair

Bibliography

Historical Embroidery

Opus Anglicanum   The Arts Council, London
Needlework, an illustrated history   Harriet Bridgeman and Elizabeth Drury
   Paddington Press, London
The Needleworker's Dictionary   Pamela Clabburn   MacMillan, London
The Bayeux Tapestry   N Denny & J Filmer-Sankey   Collins, London
Crewel Embroidery   Joan Edwards   Batsford, London
Embroidery   Mary Gostelow   Marshall Cavendish, London
English Domestic Needlework   T Hughes   Abbey Library, London
English Needlework   A F Kendrick   Black, London
English Embroidery   A F Kendrick   Newnes, Sevenoaks, Kent
Textile Collections of the World   ed. Cecil Lubell   Studio Vista, London
The Art of Cutwork and Appliqué   Herta Puls   Batsford, London,
   Brandford, Boston, Massachusetts
The Art of Embroidery   M Schuette   Thames & Hudson, London
English Historical Embroidery   Barbara Snook   Mills and Boon, London
Guide to English Embroidery   P Wardle   Victoria and Albert Museum,
   London
Drawn Fabric Embroidery   Edna Wark   Batsford, London
Embroidery Magazine   Journal of the Embroiderer's Guild, London

Costume and Armour

Costume Cavalcade   H Hansen   Methuen, London
Costumes Through the Ages   James Laver   Thames & Hudson, London
Arms and Armour   F Wilkinson   Black, London

Drawing and Design

Introducing Drawing Techniques   Robin Capon   Batsford, London,
   Watson-Guptill, New York
Anatomy and Life Drawing   D Davy   Blandford, Poole, Dorset
Art Students' Anatomy   E Farris   Dover, New York
Drawing The Human Head   Louise Gordon   Batsford, London:
   Viking, New York
Anatomy and Figure Drawing   Louise Gordon   Batsford, London:
   Viking, New York
Introduction to the Visual Arts   Series by Harrap, London

Photography

Design in Photography   O R Croy   Focal Press, London
The Photographer's Handbook   J Hedgecoe   Ebury Press, London
Effects and Experiments in Photography   P Petzold   Focal Press, London

General

The World of M C Escher   Harry Abrams Inc   New English Library,
   London
The Selective Eye   C Bernier   Zwemmer, London
Primitive Art   F Boas   Dover, New York

Indian Arts in Canada   D Dickason   published by the Department of
Indian Affairs, Ottawa, Canada
Medieval Art   S Gallagher   Tudor, New York
Oceanic Art   J Guiart   Collins, London
The Human Face   J Liggett   Constable, London
Prehistoric and Primitive Man   A Lommel   McGraw-Hill, New York
African Masks   F Monti   Paul Hamlyn, London
Celtic and Anglo-Saxon Painting   C Nordenfalk   Chatto and Windus,
London
Masks   Royal Ontario Museum, Toronto, Ontario, Canada
Celtic Mysteries   J Sharkey   Thames & Hudson, London
Grotesques and Gargoyles   Sheridan and Ross   David and Charles,
London
The Cradle of Civilization   Time-Life Books, London
African Art   F Willett   Thames & Hudson, London
The Vikings and Their Origin   D Wilson   Thames & Hudson, London

Books about the work of Henry Moore, Klimt, Picasso, Van Gogh,
Paul Klee, Hundertwasser, David Hockney, Jim Fitzpatrick,
Modigliani, etc.

Suppliers

Great Britain

General Embroidery Supplies

Mary Allen   Turnditch   Derbyshire
Art Needlework Industries Limited   7 St Michael's Mansions
   Ship Street   Oxford OX1 3DG
The Campden Needlecraft Centre   High Street   Chipping Campden
   Gloucestershire
de Denne Ltd   159–161 Kenton Road   Kenton   Harrow   Middlesex
B Francis   4 Glenworth Street   London NW1
Fresew   97 The Paddocks   Stevenage   Hertfordshire SG2 9UQ
Louis Grossé Limited   36 Manchester Street   London W1M 5PE
The Handworkers' Market   8 Fish Hill   Holt   Norfolk
Harrods Limited   London SW1
Ruth John   30 Hunts Pond Road   Park Gate   Southampton
Levencrafts   54 Church Square   Guisborough   Cleveland
MacCulloch and Wallis Limited   25–26 Dering Street
   London W1R 0BH
Mace & Nairn   89 Crane Street   Salisbury   Wiltshire
The Needlecraft Shop   corner Smallgate/Station Road   Beccles
   Suffolk
Christine Riley   53 Barclay Street   Stonehaven   Kincardineshire
   Scotland
Royal School of Needlework   25 Princes Gate   Kensington SW7 1QE
The Silver Thimble   33 Gay Street   Bath
J Henry Smith Limited   Park Road   Calverton   Woodborough
   nr Nottingham
Mrs Joan L Trickett   110 Marsden Road   Burnley   Lancashire

Threads and Yarns

Leonie Cox   9 St Peter's Road   Twickenham   Middlesex
Craftsman's Mark Limited   Treftnant   Denbighshire
William Hall & Company (Monsall) Limited   177 Stanley Road
   Cheadle Hulme   Cheshire
Silken Strands   33 Linksway   Gatley   Cheadle   Cheshire
Stephen Simpson Limited   Avenham Road Works   Preston
   Lancashire   *metal threads*
Texere Yarns   9 Peckover Street   Bradford   W. Yorkshire

Fabrics

Borovick's   16 Berwick Street   London W1   *all types*
Bradley Mail Order Textiles Limited   Brook Street Mill   PO Box 24
   Nelson   Lancashire
B Brown Limited   32–33 Greville Street   London EC1   *felts and
   hessians*
Dicksons and Company   Dungannon   County Tyrone   N. Ireland
   coloured scrim

Livingstone Textile Company   Bridport   Devon   *cheap fabrics,*
   scrims etc
N Lockhart and Sons Limited   Linktown Works   Kircaldy
   Scotland KY1 1QH   *evenweaves, scrim*

Waddings

Beckfoot Mill   Harden Bingley   Yorkshire

Leathers and PVC

R & A Kohnstamm Limited   Randack Tannery   Croydon Road
   Beckenham   Kent
John Milner Limited   67 Queen Street   Hitchin   Hertfordshire
   wide variety of leathers
The Tannery Shop   Gomshall Tanneries   Queen Street   Gomshall
   Surrey
Venables   Cuxham Road   Watlington   Oxfordshire   *PVC*

Suppliers in the USA

Embroidery threads and accessories

Appleton Brothers of London   West Main Road   Little Compton
   Rhode Island 02837
American Crewel Studio   Box 298   Boonton   New Jersey 07005
American Thread Corporation   90 Park Avenue   New York
Bucky King Embroideries Unlimited   Box 371   King Bros   3 Ranch
   Buffalo Star Rte   Sheriden   Wyoming 82801
Casa de las Tejedoras   1618 East Edinger   Santa Ana
   California 92705
Craft Kaleidoscope   6412 Ferguson Street   Indianapolis 46220
Dharma Trading Company   1952 University Avenue   Berkeley
   California 94704
Folklorico Yarn Co   522 Ramona Street   Palo Alto   California 94301
The Golden Eye   Box 205   Chestnut Hill   Massachusetts 02167
Head and Tails   River Forest   Illinois 60305
Leonida Leatherdale Embroidery Studio   90 East Gate   Winnipeg
   Manitoba R3C 2C3   Canada
Lily Mills   Shelby   North Carolina 28150
Sutton Yarns   2054 Yonge Street   Toronto   Ontario   Canada
Threadbenders   2260 Como Avenue   St Paul   Minnesota 55108
The Thread Shed   307 Freeport Road   Pittsburgh   Pennsylvania 15215
Yarn Depot   545 Sutter Street   San Francisco 94118   California

Index

Numbers *in italic* refer to page
numbers of illustrations